LITERARY LIFE:

A SECOND MEMOIR

Larry McMurtry

SIMON & SCHUSTER PAPERBACKS

New York · London · Toronto · Sydney

Simon & Schuster Paperbacks
A Division of Simon & Schuster, Inc.
1230 Avenue of the Americas
New York, NY 10020

First Simon & Schuster trade paperback edition May 2011

SIMON & SCHUSTER PAPERBACKS and colophon are
registered trademarks of Simon & Schuster, Inc.

For information about special discounts for bulk purchases,
please contact Simon & Schuster Special Sales at
1-866-506-1949 or business@simonandschuster.com.

The Simon & Schuster Speakers Bureau can bring authors
to your live event. For more information or to book an event,
contact the Simon & Schuster Speakers Bureau at
1-866-248-3049 or visit our website at www.simonspeakers.com.

Manufactured in the United States of America

10   9   8   7   6   5   4   3   2   1

The Library of Congress has cataloged the hardcover edition as follows:
McMurtry, Larry.
Literary life : a second memoir / Larry McMurtry.—1st Simon & Schuster hardcover ed.
p. cm.
1. McMurtry, Larry. 2. Authors, American—20th century—Biography. I. Title.
PS3563.A319Z46   2009
813'.54—dc22
[B]   2009030724
ISBN 978-1-4391-5993-4
ISBN 978-1-4391-5994-1 (pbk)
ISBN 978-1-4516-0659-1 (ebook)

For David Streitfeld

Longevities:

I have had the same postal box for sixty-seven years: Box 552, Archer City, Texas.

My family's first phone number in Archer City was 9.

On the ranch we still fed cattle out of a wagon.

I write on a typewriter.

I come, not just from a different time, but from a different era.

LITERARY LIFE:
A SECOND MEMOIR

I

As I REPORTED in *Books,* the first volume of these memoirs, I seem to have learned to read spontaneously, while playing hooky from the first grade. This occurred in 1942, when I was six. A cousin on his way to war stopped long enough at our ranch house to give me nineteen books, which I immediately started to read. In two weeks I had finished the box.

The first book I actually read was called *Sergeant Silk, the Prairie Scout*—the story had to do with the Canadian Mounties. Though there were no Mounties in our part of the country, I took them to be some type of cowboy, and there were plenty of those.

So eager was I to get that box of books read that I didn't at first realize that books had *authors*; it did not at first become apparent that actual human beings wrote them. Many years later I happened on to a second-hand copy of *Sergeant Silk* and discovered that the author's name was Robert Leighton (1859–1934), a British writer who wrote many boy's adventure stories in the mode of that Victorian master G. A. Henty. Among Robert Leighton's vast output were such promising titles as *The Land of Ju-Ju: A Tale of Benin, Under the Foeman's Flag; The Thirsty Sword,* and many other yarns I would have been happy to read. Unfortunately they weren't in my box.

Generally speaking, the authors of boy's adventure stories do not stint on wordage. In our time, startlingly, one author of boy's adventure stories, J. K. Rowling, did so well with her genre that she became as rich, if not richer, than the queen of England. G. A. Henty would probably have thought that J. K. Rowling was taking things a little too far.

What my memory seems unable to track back to is the point at which I began to consider *authors* when making a choice of what to read. I passed the question of authorship without really noticing it. I didn't know much but I did know that literature, like life, was inconsistent. Authors of many good books will sometimes lose the gift and write just as many bad books, and usually any number of middling books. Some might say that I've done that myself, although I have my defenders.

Archer City ISD did not, in the Forties and Fifties, when I was there, attract adventurous teachers—or, if a few wilder spirits showed up, they didn't last. The poets we read, year after year, were Poe, Longfellow, Whittier, with one or two Britishers, usually Keats, thrown in.

I read this poetry passively, making little attempt to connect the poem with the poet.

I was an avid bird hunter at the time and was also heavily into guns. I devoured every issue of *Field & Stream* and its competitors. My favorite writers, during this period, would all have been hunting writers: Elmer Keith, Jack O'Connor, and the big-game expert, Colonel Townsend Whelen.

If I had been confronted at this level with Yeats, Eliot, Hardy, Whitman, or Frost, I don't know what I would have felt.

If we exempt boy's books, hunting books, and the occasional Mickey Spillane paperback, my real reading life may be said to have begun when

I entered the Rice Institute (as it was then called) in the fall of 1954. I strolled in wonder through the stacks of Fondren Library, which then held about 600,000 books. I took freshman English under Professor Will Dowden, who had us read "The Love Song of J. Alfred Prufrock," which, at a stroke, blotted out all the poetry I had read in high school, except maybe Keats. I learned about Eliot, and the other modern poets soon followed.

At this point I had no inkling that I might, someday, be able to write books myself; and, even if I had the inkling, I would not have had the time. For me to be at Rice at all required a great intellectual leap. Just getting my homework read was all—and sometimes more than all—that I could get done.

My three roommates, in the garage apartment we lived in on North Boulevard, were, like most of the other undergraduates at Rice, studying to be engineers. Math 101 caused no trouble for my roommates; for myself it was a barrier reef I knew I would never cross—almost before I got my clothes unpacked at Rice I knew I would soon be leaving; a year and a half later, I left.

During the year and a half I was at Rice on my first pass, I didn't have time to check many books out of Fondren, but the one that made the biggest impression on me was the Italian polymath Mario Praz's *The Romantic Agony*, his study of literary decadence, mostly nineteenth-century.

From Praz I learned much about a great many writers I had previously never heard of, including the Marquis de Sade, though I can't recall that Praz mentioned that the obsessed Marquis died while copulating with a goose (if, in fact, he did).

The Romantic Agony is certainly an odd book for an uneducated eighteen-year-old yokel to pluck out of a 600,000-volume library. And yet I *did* read it, more than once. From that book, for reasons obscure to me, my serious reading started. Later on I got my own copy and have it still. (I'm a fastidious bookman and have never liked reading books with library markings or other messy defects.)

In *The Romantic Agony* Praz spends a good deal of time analyzing a now forgotten Gothic novel called *Melmoth the Wanderer*, by the Reverend Charles Robert Maturin. For Praz that book focused many Gothic tendencies. I soon found out that Rice had a copy—but it was in the rare book room and, being a mere freshman, I doubted that the librarians would allow me in this sanctuary.

In this instance I was wrong about the librarians, one of whom took me into a dark little room and turned on the light.

Melmoth the Wanderer was in three volumes, and the Rice copy was bound in boards. I was so impressed I could barely breathe.

The kindly librarian, though, was breathing fine, and at once went back to her duties, leaving me alone with this treasure.

I began to read, and then I stopped. I had never read, or even touched, a book that old, and was unprepared to appreciate what I found. To me the prose seemed turgid, but I didn't want to give up, not since the Rice librarians showed such confidence in me.

Soon enough, though, I *did* give up. *Melmoth the Wanderer* may embody all the Gothic elements Mario Praz mentioned but it was still too much for me. (Much later I owned H. P. Lovecraft's copy of *Melmoth the Wanderer*, in the attractive three-volume Bentley reprint, a book that proved much easier to sell than to read.)

Years later I read a little appreciation of Mario Praz by Edmund Wilson; the two met occasionally. From Wilson I gathered that Praz was a great historian of furniture whose Rome apartment was packed with goodies. I think it may have been Praz who turned Wilson on to the monster garden of Bomarzo, a tiny place just off the road to Orvieto. A humpbacked count had had the sculpures made. I have been there and can confirm that the sculptures are a little weird.

Perhaps even weirder is that a novel called *Bomarzo* was edited by my own longtime editor, Michael Korda, the author being Manuel Mujica Láinez, an Argentine who died in 1984. There is also an opera about Bomarzo, for which the author wrote the libretto.

As my freshman year was ending my English professor, Will Dowden, required his students to write a theme about almost any literary subject we might want to take on. For reasons now obscure, I chose to write about William Morris and the Kelmscott Press. How did I happen to know about William Morris, the Kelmscott Press, and the famous edition of Chaucer that the Press published to considerable, though, in my view, misplaced fame?

My best guess, now, is that I came to know Morris and his printing by reading the now forgotten books of a man named William Dana Orcutt. One title by Orcutt that I still recall is *In Quest of the Perfect Book*. William Dana Orcutt was just the person to be wowed by the Kelmscott *Chaucer*, which is not, to my mind, anything like the perfect book. Its text has to fight its way through the rather clotted ornamentation. Morris, in my opinion, had more skill with his wallpapers than he did with books. Various of his contemporaries did cleaner, more elegant work, particularly T. J. Cobden Sanderson at the Doves Press, whose type Sanderson eventually committed to the Thames.

Still, the Kelmscott Press served very well as a subject for a freshman theme. Will Dowden, who became my colleague, liked the paper so much that he mentioned that perhaps I ought to consider taking George Williams's creative writing class.

At this point I had never heard of creative writing. I asked Will Dowden about it and he surmised that I would be let to write short stories or poems in the class, or maybe even a play, if I cared to take that leap.

Though I had no reason to think I could become a creative writer, I was hot to try it—it was bound to be better than sitting in math class, watching the calculus sail over my head. Unfortunately a different sort of barrier arose—only upperclassmen were allowed to attempt creative writing, at least under George Williams's eye, a more complicated thing than letting a kid from West Texas into the rare book room.

Oddly enough, despite seventeen years at Rice in various roles, I never technically became an upperclassman and so did not take George Williams's writing class. As a graduate student I was above it, and, as a lecturer-professor even further above it. Besides, by the time I returned to Rice in 1963 I had published two books and was too senior for the class.

What I did take with George Williams, when I was a candidate for the MA, was his graduate course in Chaucer. George was a kindly man, with whom I developed an easy friendship. He had published one novel, *The Blind Bull*, and that effort seemed to exhaust his interest in fiction—or at least all fiction except *The Canterbury Tales*.

George Williams's passion, really, was for bird migration; he wrote on this subject for various ornithological journals. Many species migrate to the Gulf Coast, so George was kept busy by their arrivals and departures. One healthy species which migrated a little too close to Rice was the ubiquitous purple grackle, which, year after year, covered the sidewalks on campus with their rich guano. When I was first at Rice a small army of Mexican bird clappers were set at them, trying desperately to keep the sidewalks guano-free. The bird clappers were not especially successful in their effort, but they did provide a kind of medieval element to the grace-ful Moorish quadrangle around which Rice was built.

Though I didn't gain entry to George Williams's writing class, the notion of being a writer, even a creative writer, had taken root in me. I couldn't read *Melmoth the Wanderer*, but pretty soon, I made contact with the work of another wanderer, Jack Kerouac, whose effect on me, not to men-tion American letters, I'll get to in good time.

2

FOR MUCH OF my adult life I've been tempted, sporadically, to visit for-tune-tellers, just to get their opinion on my prospects, as it were. My fa-vorite of these seers and far-seers was a French woman in Tucson who kept a rather ill-tempered old goose by her side as she worked.

Over the years I've been to probably fifty fortune-tellers, in many cities and several countries. Their opinions about my romantic prospects were mixed, but about my economic prospects their opinions never varied: you'll never be rich and you'll never be poor, they always insisted—they being card readers, hand readers, seers who went into trances, clairvoy-ants and hypnotists.

So unvarying was this assurance that I'd never be either rich or poor that I took the fortune-tellers at their word and mostly give little thought to money. I have, at times, made a lot of it, though never enough to allow my money to support me. It never has and it ain't gonna, but I've always hung on to just enough to validate the judgment of the many seers I have listened to.

Money has played a fairly minor part in my career decisions, a fact I attribute to one particular piece of luck: my novels attract good filmmak-ers, and they have from the first. Nearly a dozen of my books have been filmed, four of them very successfully: *Hud*, *The Last Picture show*, *Terms of Endearment*, and *Lonesome Dove*.

9

The success of these films, whether or not I took any part in their production, has enabled to me to get work as a screenwriter—and get it consistently for over fifty years.

Screenwriting, not novel writing, has funded my rare bookshop and, to a large extent, my so far comfortable life.

My transfer, in January of 1955, from Rice Institute to North Texas State Teachers College (as they were then) could not easily have been less auspicious. The weather in North Texas, where I was heading, had been warm and drizzly, but then the temperature took a forty degree plunge, turning the road to Dallas into a sheet of ice. Such storms are not uncommon in North Texas, and the closer one is to Amarillo the worse they get. On this trip I slid off the road twice, but managed to slip and slide back on.

When I reached Dallas I was navigating through a two-inch ice-free hole on my windshield. There was then no arching confluence of freeways to guide me through Dallas—in fact there was nothing to guide me anywhere. By some miracle, while right downtown, I managed to spot the Hotel Adolphus, where I took a room for the night. The Adolphus—where, later, I would make a speech or two—was the most elegant hotel I had ever stayed in, although the famous Baker Hotel in Mineral Wells, where my rich Panhandle uncles wintered, ran a close second.

In the morning I slipped and slid into Denton, quickly found a room, and took myself off to the registrar, where the first thing I did was register for a creative writing course taught by a professor named James Brown. North Texas State was, at the time, a big messy school, with a student body drawn from the suburbs of Fort Worth, Dallas, and Oklahoma City. Lots of veterans were about, finishing their education on the GI Bill. There was a flourishing jazz school there, and the faculty was filled with smart young professors from the great Midwestern universities.

In this case there was no "upperclassmen only" policy. Jim Brown, who became a friend, let in such students as wanted in; a good many did but the room where Jim taught was never full.

Most American creative writing programs in that time proceeded from an obviously mistaken theory, the theory being that it is easier to write something short than to write something long. The exact opposite is true: the lyric poem remains the most difficult form, with the short story next; the novel is, for most writers, the least difficult form.

I'm sure Jim Brown knew this, but the class only ran one semester and very few novels are likely to be written between January and May—although I have written four in less time than that.

So we wrote short stories, a form I never came close to mastering. I couldn't write them and I seldom read them. The only short story I could claim to have read at the time was Frank R. Stockton's "The Lady, or the Tiger?" Such masters as Hemingway, Faulkner, Sherwood Anderson, Katherine Anne Porter, or distant giants such as Chekhov, Flaubert, Maupassant, and D. H. Lawrence, were as yet completely beyond my ken.

Despite this dreadful lack of background I nonetheless produced sixty-three short stories during my two and a half years in Denton. All were dreadful and all were destroyed the week before I graduated in 1958.

I did later publish, in the *Texas Quarterly*, a half-decent short story called "There Will Be Peace in Korea," a title I stole from the gospel singer Sister Rosetta Tharpe. The story was in fact a kind of précis of *The Last Picture Show*. The actor Tommy Lee Jones has done a reading of it that is very fine; it makes the story seem better than it is.

Jim Brown, like all creative writing teachers, read and listened to a vast amount of bad student writing, a fact that didn't seem to disturb him—it surely came with the territory. The only comment I can recall him making on something I turned in was to mildly chide me for an inaccuracy—I had used the phrase "soft white hands of a dentist." Jim pointed out that while most dentists' hands were white, few were soft, their main function, after all, being to yank or wrench resistant teeth out of their sockets.

Other than Jim Brown three other professors at North Texas attempted to awaken me in their various ways. One, the philosopher and film theorist Bill Linden, is still alive and still a friend. Bill guided me through the giddy heights of Hegel, and seemed to be the only person around who knew something about Existentalism. Eventually he glided back into the University of Illinois system, his perch being at Edwardsville.

Such American literature as I was taught arrived via the flamboyant personage of Martin Shockley, a Coloradan who insisted on keeping the classroom windows open no matter what the weather.

A somber professor named Ballard taught us what most of us were to know about the continental novel; we read Balzac, Turgenev, Flaubert, Tolstoy, and maybe Gogol. I think I even read a few easy pieces—Daudet, perhaps—in my stumbling French, which still stumbles in about the same degree. I would never try to employ it in conversation, or on a hard text such as Proust.

During my stay at North Texas three poets came to visit: Paul Engle, May Sarton, and the poet-publisher Jonathan Williams, who created and ran the wonderful Jargon Press. As a bookseller I handled many Jargon books, all of which appealed to me more than the Kelmscott *Chaucer*. (Engle and Williams I'm sure about—I may have hallucinated May Sarton, who may not have been there at all.)

From this period, precisely, I date my entrance into the scrappy, variegated world of letters. None of these poet-visitors were then very famous— if they had been famous they probably would not have been visiting this scruffy little teacher's college. But they *were* writers. Engle, at the time I believe, ran the famous writing program at the University of Iowa; Sarton eventually enjoyed a substantial readership; and Jonathan Williams's Jargon was one of the two or three best small presses of our time.

To a beginning writer such as myself even the slightest literary ferment was good. Professors, book editors, reviewers, journalists, book salesmen, fellow beginners, authors of first books, girl (and boy) friends and mistresses of all the above, drew me in and made me believe that this was a game I could have a part in; at the very least I could teach.

It was Jim Brown's creative writing class that led me into this diverse world, and I was lucky to study under him just when I did, because I think he was teaching that class for the last, or maybe next to last time.

While I'm at it, I should emphasize that my path to authorship was a long, stutter-step affair. Nothing about it was predetermined—I had no vision on the Damascus road. I hoped to be a writer, but it was not until I had published my *fifth* book, *All My Friends Are Going to Be Strangers*, that I became convinced that I *was* a writer and would remain one. The year before that book came out I taught my last class at Rice, where I was awarded a tenure I never really used. Marcia Carter and I had just opened our rare bookshop in Washington, D.C., and the academic life dropped behind me, forever as it turned out.

3

IT WOULD NOT do to leave a discussion of my years at North Texas without mentioning my friendship with Grover Lewis, at that time easily the most talented young writer at North Texas State. Grover was a legally blind student with a tragic past and a very questing intellect. He was one of those intellectuals—Susan Sontag was another—who somehow manage to be the first to know about any new development in the vast field of arts and letters—*any* arts and *any* letters.

It could be a new director, Kubrick, say, about whom Grover wrote the first mention I saw of the man who made *Dr. Strangelove*. Or it could be a performance artist, a collagist, a Bulgarian philosopher, or, maybe, Simone Weil. By the time I found out about these people Grover, like Susan, would have been there first.

Grover was, I believe, a genuine poet, though his output was small. So far as I'm aware there's just one booklet, *I'll Be There in the Morning if I Live*, published, I believe, by *Rolling Stone*, for whom Grover mainly worked.

He had also, by the time I met him, published a play called *Wait for Morning, Child*, a Carson McCullersesque drama which I believe was performed somewhere—I'm not sure where.

* * *

The tragic past Grover had to cope with was that his father, Big Grover, and his mother, Opel Baily Lewis, while in the midst of a fight about Big Grover's involvement with another woman, struggled for possession of a handgun Big Grover had brought back from World War II. Each, Grover then believed, shot the other dead—with eight-year-old Grover standing by. This occurred in San Antonio, where Big Grover drove a truck for the famous Pearl Brewery.

It was never clear to me whether or not this trauma caused Grover's eye condition. In any case his eyeballs jiggled, though most of his friends ceased to notice this.

As to the killings, Jan Reid and W. K. Stratton, who edited *Splendor in the Short Grass*, Grover's posthumously published last book, suggest that after Big Grover shot Grover's mother five times, he dropped the pistol, at which point an old man who was there cleaning the bathroom picked up the gun and shot Big Grover dead. At any rate Big Grover died and the old man cleaning the bathroom was never prosecuted.

It's been my fortune to know three writers who handily acquired disciples: Grover Lewis, Billy Lee Brammer, and Ken Kesey. The latter, of course, had a little band of disciples called the Merry Pranksters. Their king is dead but remnants of the tribe still exist.

Of the three writers, two, Billy Lee and Grover, lived in my houses, in Austin and Houston, during times when their fortunes were at a low ebb. My young son, James, knew all three of these writers, though not well.

Grover Lewis found his disciples one or two at a time. I doubt any of them thought of themselves *as* disciples, but I know that I offend those who survive, by suggesting—it seemed to me obvious—that Grover fictionalized his journalism, much of which was produced in the Sixties and Seventies for *Rolling Stone*, never, in my opinion, exactly a bastion of literalism. I probably knew Grover's work better than I knew him, and to me it is hard to imagine Grover writing any prose that he did not fictionalize.

A particularly clear example of what I mean can be found in the title essay of his last book, *Splendor in the Short Grass*, Grover's piece about the making of *The Last Picture Show*, in which he claims that he and I stood in the parking lot of a honky-tonk in Wichita Falls, Texas, and watched Elvis Presley have a fight with a roughneck. Here are my areas of dispute:

A. I was never in or near a honky-tonk in Wichita Falls with Grover. In *2005* I was in a honky-tonk in Wichita Falls with Ang Lee and a few others scouting locations for *Brokeback Mountain*; but never previously.

B. I never saw Elvis Presley live. He did perform in Wichita Falls but way after my time.

C. I was never in any honky-tonk with Grover, ever.

D. Later in the essay Grover reports that an AD (Assistant Director) called his crew to order with the words "Let us now praise famous men"— a line from Ecclesiasticus and also, of course, the title of a famous book by James Agee and Walker Evans with which Grover had a complex history, related later. That an AD on a movie set in Archer City, Texas, would summon his crew with those words was exactly the kind of thing Grover made up, not in that one essay but over and over again. It's even more unlikely than the Elvis episode.

When I met Grover he was working on a long story called "Their Mouths No Longer Drink." The epitaph is from Bartok, and the tone of that story is very much like the tone of much of Grover's journalism.

17

LARRY MCMURTRY

Grover and I both published in the North Texas State college magazine, which was called *Avesta*. Grover's stories and poems were a lot better
than my stories and poems, though neither of us rose very high.

As we were approaching graduation, in May of 1958, we decided over
dinner to publish a short magazine of our own. It consisted of fragments
of things the two of us were working on, plus similar fragments from
friends.

To accomplish this publication, which was called *The Coexistence Review*, we made free use of the English Department Xerox machine. The
first issue was printed on ordinary white bond, but for the second issue
we got a little fancier and switched to an art paper of some kind. On the
cover was a big red star. I naively saw nothing wrong with this, and, indeed, there *was* nothing wrong with it except the timing. As a rancher's
son, raised in West Texas, I had grown up so far beyond the reach of Mc-
Carthyism that I was only dimly aware of it. At the time I may not have
even heard of Stalin. But, at the college, it did cause a rustling in the dove-
cotes, such as they were.

I don't know that anything very severe actually happened as a result of
this piece of student mischief, but I think it cast a little bit of a pall over
Jim Brown's career, although we were not his students when we printed
the two issues of our little magazine. Fortunately, when Jim left Denton,
he left for the University of Illinois, where he eventually became chancel-
lor of, I believe, the whole state system.

The last few times I saw Jim Brown it was in Washington, where he had
come to lobby for his schools.

I liked and admired Grover Lewis, and, rube though I was, I understood
from the first that he was a complex man. He was a polished writer long
before I had ever written a single sentence worth publishing, or read-

18

ing. The first inkling I had that he had somewhat complex feelings about me—they wouldn't have been unusual among young writers anywhere—came at a party in 1959, when I was in Denton, visiting.

During my years there I had continued to make reading lists of books I really wanted to read. Our own Ben Franklin did much the same. At the top of my list, for a very long time, was *Let Us Now Praise Famous Men*, the extraordinary study of the tenant farmer system, done at the bidding of *Fortune* magazine, by James Agee and Walker Evans—the latter, of course, took the pictures.

The North Texas State library had a copy of *Let Us Now Praise Famous Men*, but it was checked out and stayed checked out for a whole year. At the party in 1959 Grover somewhat sheepishly showed the book to me—he had had it all along. It was at that point that I stopped thinking of him simply as a friend, though we continued to see one another for most of the Sixties. And I'll repeat my point that it was very unlikely that the AD on *Picture Show*, helping film my book in my hometown, ever used that phrase or even knew that anyone ever had. (Unless Grover, who was there both as an actor and a reporter, put him up to it.)

Grover taught for a time in Lubbock, where I visited him once; what I remember from that meeting was that sometime during the inevitable party the novelist John Rechy showed up. This would have been, I think, before John's first novel, *City of Night*, was published but not before the Pershing Square segment, called "The Fabulous Wedding of Miss Destiny" had appeared, bringing John Rechy instant, if rather specialized, fame. That night, at Grover's, he was wearing his leather traveling clothes, and gave us all a start.

(Once, passing through El Paso, where John Rechy lived with his mother, I spent a pleasant afternoon driving around with John, looking for a beer joint where they might mistake him for an underaged teenager and ask to see his ID. In a recent interview someone mentioned that John Rechy was *cheerful* about his narcissism. When *City of Night* did come out I reviewed it favorably for *The Washington Post*.)

In 1955 or '56 Grover stayed with James and me on Quenby Street for a while. Sometime in the summer he experienced a serious disappointment in love and, soon after, left town. I never saw him with any frequency again but I kept up with him through mutual friends, and, of course, through his writing. A first collection of his journalism called *Academy All the Way* was published in 1974. There was also a strange single-sheet fold-over from about this time; it was called *The Last Poem: All My Friends Are Going to Be Published*, a riposte, I guess, to my own *All My Friends Are Going to Be Strangers*. But an odd riposte.

The last time I saw Grover, after a gap of at least twenty years, was in Dutton's Bookshop on San Vicente, Brentwood. My writing partner, Diana Ossana, and I were signing copies of our collaborative novel *Pretty Boy Floyd* when Grover and his wife Rae showed up in the line and bought a copy. We chatted politely for about a minute and then the Lewises were gone, as are, alas, the Dutton bookshops. Grover's first wife and his last seemed to be very nice women—in between marriages he was not so fortunate.

The writer Dave Hickey, who became a friend of Grover's, contributed a lovely tribute in *Splendor in the Short Grass*, and Grover's friends Jan Reid and W. K. Stratton added a helpful introduction.

The piece on the making of *Picture Show* pleased no one who had worked on the film, nor did his piece on the Allman Brothers please the Allman Brothers band. (Duane Allman had been killed in a motorcycle accident before the piece appeared.)

Journalists mostly don't expect to be liked—*Vanity Fair* is not paying its writers big money to write nice things about their subjects.

But I stand by my conviction that Grover Lewis essentially wrote fiction.

I feel he anticipated and then participated with the New Journalism—Tom Wolfe, David Halberstam, Gay Talese, Marshall Frady, Hunter S. Thompson, and others; these writers employed the techniques of fiction while banking on the stronger appeal of fact. Grover was one of them.

He died of lung cancer not long after I encountered him in Dutton's now lost and gone bookshop. I still remember how excited I was by Grover's first poems, particularly by a poem called "In Loco Parentis" which I reread recently and still find powerful. It seems to be a kind of anticipation of the conflict that took his parents.

A few years before he died Grover began to sell a few of his books. His copies of *The Coexistence Review* went to a New York collector; where they reside now I'm not sure. I ran into the copy of *Leaving Cheyenne* I had inscribed to him, bought it back, and scribbled a gibberish inscription which greatly increased its value.

A rule of the ages is that when people need money they sell what they have on hand. Thousands of booksellers have profited by this fact.

There can, though, be other reasons for parting with books or objects, the simplest being that the person may no longer want to be reminded of the time or circumstance the *objet* represents. I long ago, as a collected author, came to accept this. Probably at least 85 percent of the books I've inscribed both to friends and strangers have found their way into the market, and often rather rapidly. (I recently bought a book that one well-known Texas figure had inscribed to another well-known Texas figure—it had taken only three days for the book to be given, inscribed, and then sold to me, 265 miles up the highway.)

But, that's the book biz. I myself sold my mother's copies of some of my early books, and why not? Both parents are dead and siblings were fully supplied with my books. So off Mom's books went, at least one of them snatched by the dedicatee of this memoir.

I should restate one obvious point: young writers are competitive with one another. I was competitive in turn with Grover Lewis, Bill Brammer, and Ken Kesey. Norman Mailer's recently published letters demonstrate what had long been known: that he and Styron and James Jones were competitive with one another. This is about as surprising as that Picasso was jealous of Matisse, and vice versa. And the younger the writers the more intense the rivalry will be.

I discovered this factor most forcibly in my friendship with Ken Kesey, who had been a wrestler before he became a writer. Ken was a very competitive writer when I met him; he really *had* to be the stud duck. We met in the famous Stegner class at Stanford in 1960, a class he clearly intended to dominate and more or less did dominate although the competition was tougher than he supposed it would be.

Twenty-five years later, by chance, I won a Pulitzer Prize for *Lonesome Dove*, after which my times with Ken were never quite the same. In time, if he had continued to write, he probably would have won a Pulitzer too.

I now think that the wrinkle in our friendship had been there before my Pulitzer, and had to do with the fact that I had kept writing and he had (mainly) stopped. Once I asked him directly if he intended to write any more novels and he sort of shrugged. "If you've made two fairly high mountains why make a third?" he said.

Ken Kesey had a big talent, and I think, in time, came to regret not continuing with fiction. *Spit in the Ocean*, the journal he edited irregularly with Ken Babbs, was trivial even by Prankster standards, which were not high. It may be too that the two mountains he had built were perhaps not quite as high as he had at first believed. (I am one of the minority who think the second book, *Sometimes a Great Notion*, is a better book than *Cuckoo's Nest*, but that could be because I heard *Cuckoo's Nest* read aloud in class, whereas the second book I reviewed and read carefully.)

Sailor Song, the book Ken Kesey wrote when he returned to the writing trade, is a pretty good novel, but it lacks the terrific metaphoric force of the earlier books.

4

In the spring of 1958, just as I was about to receive my BA, I applied to several graduate schools, with the intent of working toward a graduate degree in English. I got two offers, Rice and the University of Illinois, Urbana. With no Math 101 to bedevil me, I chose Rice. My first stay in Houston had not been long enough. I was eager to go back. I knew that the program I would be entering was an old-fashioned Johns Hopkins–style graduate program, with a certain amount of philology involved.

The stipend Rice was offering then was minute, but it was enough.

By this time I knew that I really wanted to be a writer. I had spent the summer pounding out a rough draft of *Horseman, Pass By*, and by early fall, when I had plunged deep into graduate studies, I had also raced through an even rougher draft of *Leaving Cheyenne*, which, years later, became my second novel.

The first book, *Horseman, Pass By*, is about the destruction of a ranching family after its herd had been destroyed out of fears of hoof-and-mouth. *Horseman, Pass By*, is of course the famous last line of the epitaph of William Butler Yeats. Mary McCarthy took the first line for her novel *Cast a Cold Eye*.

Here's the whole epitaph:

Cast a cold Eye
On Life, on Death.
Horseman, pass by

Certainly the fact that I had two novels in draft already gave me a leg up on my fellow graduate students, with the exception of the prolific John William Corrington, a poet, novelist, and firebrand from Louisiana whom I never knew really well. (With his wife, Joyce, a Rice Ph.D. in [I believe] chemistry, the Corringtons helped create *General Hospital*, the immensely popular soap.) Bill Corrington died young, but not before producing an impressive body of work.

Among the new graduates in English arriving at Rice with me were Ray and Linda Waddington, who lived in a trailer camp on South Main, not far from school. We soon became friends and remained friends for years. Ironically they had come to Houston from Stanford, where—though I didn't know it yet—I was about to go. They had even lived on the famous short bohemian street, Perry Lane, and had in fact moved out of the house the Keseys would soon move into.

From the Waddingtons I gleaned much gossip about Stanford—but since I then had no notion that I would ever go there I didn't absorb it until much later. Yvor Winters, who ran the poetry program while Wallace Stegner ran the fiction, loomed a lot larger in the Waddingtons' view than Ken Kesey. (I often saw the magisterial Yvor Winters crossing the campus, but never met him, nor did I meet his brilliant wife, the poet and novelist Janet Lewis, until, a long time later, I sought her out and wrote a piece about her. She was then in her ninety-eighth year; she died just short of the century, which she had hoped to reach.)

*   *   *

The Waddingtons soon came under the sway of the newly arrived Miltonist, Jackson I. Cope, who brought what might be called the New Scholarship to Rice. I often saw Jack Cope walking the campus with his perfectly groomed collie and his beautiful, also perfectly groomed, wife.

Jack Cope drove his graduate students a good deal harder than graduate students at Rice were used to being driven. Since I never took his Milton seminar I was unaffected by his behavior, and did not run with him, box with him, or accompany him to the gym where Sonny Liston was then in training for his disastrous bout with young Cassius Clay (later Muhammad Ali).

I took Cope book scouting once or twice, on Washington Avenue, but since what he mainly collected was Italian drama of the Renaissance, not much of which made its way to Houston, these excursions bored us both.

Cope soon drifted back to Hopkins, then to USC, then back to Hopkins again, how officially I don't know. He was a small man who occasionally liked to pretend to be a mafioso. (His effect on his graduate students was a little Godfather-like.) By curious chance I had lunch in Baltimore with Jack Cope the day before my heart surgery.

Like Bill Corrington, Jackson I. Cope died young, in manner if not in years.

5

I DON'T THINK I've ever been happier than during my first graduate year at Rice: 1958–1959 that would be. Rice was so trusting in those days that graduate students were given keys to the library, though I seemed to be one of the few who took daily or nightly advantage of this privilege. I romanticized my nocturnal ramblings around that comfortable library in *All My Friends*. I never slept in Fondren, as my character Danny Deck did—I had no need to, since my apartment was right across Rice Boulevard, five minutes away.

But I wandered the library constantly. In the early evening I would usually take a break and saunter across the vast stadium parking lot to eat a modest meal at a cafeteria in what is still called The Village, after which I would walk back across the same parking lot toward the spires of Rice (well, one spire at least, the famous Campanile). In those days Rice had only about half as many buildings as it has now—the same can be said for the great Medical Center, just across South Main from the school.

Then Rice had a lot of open space. One could see fine cloudscapes from the lights of the city, or watch airplanes angling down toward Hobby Airport. I loved that walk, but if I tried it today I'd see a very different cityscape. The vast Med Center, plus the many new buildings that have sprung up at Rice, form a kind of urban massif.

What one senses is the huge, still increasing, power of Houston, which keeps throwing up buildings, suburbs, freeways.

I spoke at Rice recently and was forced to admit that I knew neither the school nor the city very well. Since Houston was my first city, and I was in and out of it for seventeen years, as student, professor, bookseller, this knowledge of my ignorance is a little saddening. It remains, by a large measure, the most interesting city in Texas and going there stirs a lot of memories.

As I was writing this memoir word came that John Updike died—a great man of letters is gone. I met him years ago, when he and I and Annie Dillard were on a panel. Updike was then sort of quietly collecting his onetime colleague E. B. White. I quickly supplied him with a nice copy of *Every Day Is Saturday* and tried to initiate a bit of a correspondence, which, after only two letters, he politely cut off.

Considering the vastness of his output in a number of genres, plus the fact that he made his living writing, it is no wonder that he had no time for extended correspondence with someone he would probably never see again.

I think, as in the case of his friend Joyce Carol Oates, Updike's very output worked against him a little. He wrote so much that even nominally keeping up was a full-time job.

That, late in his career, he and Mailer both attacked Tom Wolfe is odd. Why? Tom Wolfe, a friendly man, barked back, but not uncivilly or even very loudly.

I gave John Updike a very good price on *Every Day Is Saturday*, and he chided me a little, in what turned out to be our last contact.

My only trip to Houston's great Med Center was to take my son to have his tonsils out, in the mid-Sixties. The relevance of this information is slight, but, by chance, the famed surgeon Denton Cooley was performing the first American heart transplant in the same hospital on the same day—he was using, as it happened, a device he borrowed from the even more celebrated heart surgeon Michael DeBakey, recently deceased but not before he attained his hundredth year. Dr. Cooley's use of the "device" led to one of the most famous feuds in medical history. Happily the two divas made up shortly before DeBakey's death.

My own memory of this momentous occasion is that, with such world-shaking events going on, it took an awfully long time to get anyone to pay attention to my son's bleeding throat.

For a time in the late Fifties and early Sixties, graduate school, for the literary-minded, was briefly the place to be. The Korean War was over; Vietnam had not yet heated up. Journalism was soon to become an attractive and a lucrative place to be, but the New Journalists who propelled it—Tom Wolfe, David Halberstam, Marshall Frady, Larry L. King, Gay Talese, Hunter S. Thompson, and others—had not yet collectively kicked in.

So, in that time, people such as myself settled for graduate school. Though thousands took this path, graduate school never became a popular subject for fiction. There's Philip Roth's *Letting Go*, my own *Moving On*, and that's about it. At the time I don't think I realized that I was living a highly specialized life, a life which mainly just required me to read. I was friendly with the new purists of the Cope faction but I was more comfortable with old-fashioned scholars such as Alan McKillop and Will Dowden.

If I was uncomfortable at all during this period it was because I knew well enough that I wasn't a scholar and would never become one. After all, I had those two novel manuscripts in my drawer, which meant that I had options my fellow graduate students, Bill Corrington excepted, just didn't have.

All my teachers were good, but the only one who really said anything useful to the writer I would become was Alan Dugald McKillop, with whom I read the English novel.

At the end of our term, the McKillops felt obliged to bring the students in the novel class over for tea. They lived in a modest home on West University Place. It proved to be a rather stiff occasion—neither of the McKillops was rich in small talk. But one thing Alan McKillop said stuck in my mind. "If I were going to write a novel," he said, "I'd be sure to know the history of the genre before I attempted to add to it."

That seemed like sound advice, sound enough that I soon set out to read the English novel from Samuel Richardson to Anthony Powell—the latter being by then well launched on his *A Dance to the Music of Time* sequence, twelve volumes of which eventually appeared.

I think I saw a few volumes of Anthony Powell on the McKillops' shelves, but I saw even more volumes of the academic novels of C. P. Snow, whom McKillop regarded as having at least a slight edge on Anthony Powell. (I wouldn't have agreed then, but I might agree now.)

Reflecting back across half a century to Alan McKillop's sensible assertion about knowing the genre one plans to work in, I went into the long unvisited room in my library where I keep histories of literature—I used to read them for pleasure.

There I discovered that I owned and had mostly read *160* books about the novel: histories, critiques, theories, casual essays, practitioners' memoirs, etc. These led me to recall that I once had been engrossed by literary theory when it applied to the novel. I enjoyed sensible, plain commentary, such as one finds in E. M. Forster's *Aspects of the Novel,* as well as the highly colored didactic work of Georg Lukács and others.

At some point I even read the famous prefaces that Henry James used to introduce the various volumes of the impressive New York Edition of his major fictions.

The Prefaces, I feel, were mainly useful to James himself, as he tried to explain, for readers of the New York Edition, exactly what he had once attempted in his fiction, and why he attempted it. In my opinion the same writer's *Notebooks* are, as a manual of practice, more useful; and better still, I think, are the hundreds of reviews of French and English fiction that Henry James wrote over a long working career as a reviewer.

Mr. James, like Mr. Updike, was *never* an amateur. From the first, like Updike, James took reviewing seriously. Both writers' reviews, all done for hire, contain some of their most brilliant observations.

To James and Updike I would add the reviews of Virginia Woolf, who also wrote for money and gave extremely good value for that money, which was, for some years, quite modest.

When I began to write novels the most admired work of theory, where prose fiction was concerned, was probably Percy Lubbock's *The Craft of Fiction*. In my view, as a critic of fiction, Lubbock is pretty much Henry James writ small.

Of my 160 books on the novel the only ones I return to are F. R. Leavis's *The Great Tradition*, and his wife, Q. D. Leavis's, *Fiction and the Reading Public*, adding, for its brilliance, D. H. Lawrence's *Studies in Classic American Literature*.

Lawrence will probably endure, and the Leavises fade. F. R. Leavis, for one thing, was a better critic of poetry than he was of the novel.

I also enjoyed, about that time, a collection of R. P. Blackmur's studies of the European novel, which brought Tolstoy into my life—he is lodged there still.

6

_____

IN THE SUMMER of 1958 I opened an envelope one day and discovered that I had had two poems accepted by *Southwest Review*: my first actual acceptance by a real, grown-up magazine. For the very first time I began to feel that I might be a writer. I was so thrilled that I went out into the burning streets of Archer City—115 degrees that day—and took a long, triumphant walk.

One of the poems was to the photographer Erwin E. Smith, whose photographs of the early days of cowboying on the Texas range leave a wonderful record of a vanished way of life; my poem about Erwin Smith was actually pretty good.

7

WHAT MY 160 critical books on the novel remind me now is that I grew up intellectually at the end of an age of criticism. It was a time, as the witty poet-critic Randall Jarrell observed, when every swan wanted to be a duck.

In addition to Jarrell—a splendid reviewer and anthologist—we had Eliot and Pound, an era in themselves, as well as Ransom, Tate, Kenneth Burke, Edmund Wilson, Yvor Winters, and, from England, I. A. Richards, William Empson, the Leavises, V. S. Pritchett, and others. I myself read, or tried to read, those critics and all the others mentioned in Stanley Edgar Hyman's once important book *The Armed Vision*, his study of modern criticism, which I read and reread until he came out with a second book I liked even better, that being *The Tangled Bank*, his study of Darwin, Marx, Frazer, and Freud. It was on the whole a painstaking effort, but one from which I learned a great deal.

I read this criticism avidly, although I was by then aware that the age of criticsm was ending or had ended. Northrop Frye's *Anatomy of Criticism*, the most important critical book published during my academic years, was also one of the last critical works to really engage me.

For day-to-day reading I preferred the practical, workaday critics such as Edmund Wilson or V. S. Pritchett. And, a little later, John Updike.

The events, however, which in my generation made a lot of homely ducks wish to turn back into swans were the publications, in 1956 and 1957 respectively, of *Howl* and *On the Road*, about which more later. The two books opened wide the gates through which soon pushed the New Journalists, with Tom Wolfe then leading the pack, and, more importantly the Black Humorists (or postmodernists, if you'd rather): Nabokov, Walker Percy, Joseph Heller, Barthelme, Barth, Pynchon, and the like.

I read both the New Journalists and the Black Humorists avidly, although I soon concluded that I was not going to be able to run with either of these packs. I was, I early became aware, an old-fashioned realist, which I have remained through the composition of twenty-nine old-fashioned novels, few of which have been much welcomed by reviewers, at least until *Lonesome Dove* came loping along.

Despite my unfashionability, which was real, I was nonetheless lucky to come along when I did, if only from the basic perspective of getting published. When I had *Horseman, Pass By* cleaned up to my own satisfaction I only had to send it out twice. One rejection slip came, and then I sent the typescript to the newly spiffed-up *Texas Quarterly*, where I found a sympathetic reader in the late Frank Wardlaw. The *Quarterly* wasn't publishing book-length manuscripts, but Frank Wardlaw sent the typescript on to an editor he knew at Harper's by the name of John Leggett, who wanted many changes but eventually optioned and published both my first novel and my second. John was a novelist as well as an editor: he accepted the book and I was launched. (In fact my first three editors, John Leggett, Bill Decker at Dial, and Michael Korda at Simon and Schuster were all novelists. I could make that four if I count Ed Doctorow, who was editor in chief at Dial at the time.)

After Dial I went to Simon and Schuster, where, except for three brief vacations, I've been ever since, under Michael Korda's rapidly beating wing.

How lucky was I to send my first novel to a smart, kindly reader, who himself took the trouble to send it up the way; and how lucky I was too to begin my career at a time when it was relatively easy to publish first novels. More than one hundred were published by trade publishers in 1961, the year I published *Horseman*. Publishers then still considered themselves to be gentlemen and scholars, and they still thought it was important to publish young writers, carrying them for a book or two until they matured and, hopefully, produced a little revenue for the firm.

8

Horseman, Pass By, written in 1958, was published in 1961, a rapid progress really. I had expected to be thrilled when I received my first copy of my first book, but when I opened the package and held the first copy in my hand, I found that I just felt sort of flat. There it was. I had made it into the ranks of the published, as I was to do about forty more times. But I felt no great surge of satisfaction. I learned then and have relearned many times since, that the best part of a writer's life is actually *doing* it, making up characters, filling the blank page, creating scenes that readers in distant places might connect to. The thrill lies in the rush of sentences, the gradual arrival of characters who at once seem to have their own life. Faulkner said that he just listens to his own characters and writes down what they say. I *watch* mine, and try, like Conrad, to make the reader *see* what's going on. You soon lose the sense, in writing fiction, that you yourself are making things happen. I wrote about Emma Horton, in the four *Terms of Endearment* books, and never once thought that I was commanding her to do this or that. When she died I felt the loss most keenly, just as, right now, I feel the loss of Duane Moore, the main character in the five *Last Picture Show* books. My final visit with Duane occurs in a novel called *Rhino Ranch*. I have now followed Duane Moore from adolescence to old age and it would be strange if I *didn't* miss him. He was not my alter ego in the first books, but he was certainly my alter ego in the last books.

I should repeat once more how lucky I was to have begun the struggle for publication at just the right time. If I had sought publication even three years later I would have walked a harder road, as, for example, did the brilliant Texas writer Max Crawford, who took seven years to get his own first novel into print. The book was called *The Backslider*—perhaps in part the delay was caused by Max's first title for this excellent novel about the hard-bitten wheat farmers of the caprock region: *The Penis of Jesus*, a title that would undoubtedly make it a hard sell in Floydada, where Max grew up.

Max Crawford had, I believe, to produce his second, no less Hobbesian, novel, *Waltz Across Texas*, before the dark but accurate *Backslider* could be published. (The fact that LBJ was president then had a braking effect on the publication of Texas fiction for several years.)

I often, at my lectures, remind would-be writers that many of the novelists and short story writers, that most of the writers they now admire most had to write two or three unpublished efforts before they finally broke through. A look back at literary history suggests that this has long been the case. Ken Kesey, for example, wrote two novels prior to *Cuckoo's Nest*. I remember reading a chapter of one called (I think) *Zoo*, about a fire in a chicken house, with flaming chickens flying all around. I believe the manuscripts of these two pre–*Cuckoo's Nest* books were destroyed by a fire in Ken's writing shack, in, I think, La Honda, California.

To this day it is not easy to get started in fiction, but the speed with which self-publishing has been established is making getting started a good deal easier. In my own hometown, where, for so long, I was the only published writer (excepting one poet and the county historian, my neighbor Jack Loftin); now there are at least three, and one of the three, Jim Black, wrote and self-published a novel called *There's a River Down in Texas* which was later picked up by Penguin, a very respectable house. Jim Black's approach to breaking in has now been repeated many times; self-publishing is obviously going to become easier and easier—and more and more common. Much trash will get published, but then much trash is published even by the most reputable publishers.

9

Michael Korda, himself an excellent and prolific author, became my editor in 1968, since which he's edited about thirty-five of my books, fiction as well as nonfiction.

After an initial phone conversation or two Michael took the trouble to come down to Houston and meet me, staying at the oilman John Meacham's elegant Warwick Hotel, just across the street from the Houston Museum of Fine Arts.

John Leggett indeed came to Texas twice, to represent the house of Harper at a couple of ill-attended autograph parties. Though never flashy, John *did* wear a suit and tie, leading me to assume, falsely, that all New York editors dressed somewhat formally, which is why it took me a while to locate Michael Korda in the Warwick's crowded bar. When, largely by a process of elimination, I did find him I faced a slim, quick young man wearing a pair of cowboy boots made for him by the great Arizona bootmaker Paul Bond, plus a shirt and vest ensemble that was top of the line but did *not* suggest the Nudies look of a faux-cowboy wearing one of that famous outfitter's required outfits.

A friend named Babette Fraser was with us this evening; she and I were both rather stunned by Michael Korda's sartorial dash. I later learned that, thanks to his schooling, which included Le Rosey, Harrow, the City of

London, and the watering places frequented by his famous, far-flung family, Michael can adapt to any social habitat, high or low, not excluding the Hungarian Revolution.

If he had to choose between high and low, Michael would probably choose low, which helped to make him the perfect editor for a skinny novelist from Archer City.

Michael and I became friends and remain friends. In his wonderful book *Charmed Lives* he describes his famous family: Sir Alexander Korda the great film producer was his uncle, as was Zoltan Korda, director of *The Four Feathers* and many other films. Vincent Korda, his father, was an Oscar-winning set designer, and his mother was a well-known actress. Thus the ground Michael walked on from birth was the most expensive ground on the planet, and the celebrities he has known and worked with are beyond count. At his long-held table in the Four Seasons Grill Room he might host Cher one day and Henry Kissinger the other; and, if Cher or Henry mislaid their calendars and showed up on the same day, Michael could swing with that too and the graceful life would go on. I doubt that there's a celebrity on earth that Michael Korda would find himself in awe of; because he was born into what became the Jet Set, his abilities to make celebrities, from presidents on down, feel at home is a gift Simon and Schuster has long depended on.

It is true, however, that a constant diet of celebrities can become too much of a good thing, which is why he enjoyed himself so much at the little Italian joint Babette and I took him to off the notoriously violent Telephone Road, which is still there (the road and the violence, not the restaurant).

My editor-author relationship with Michael Korda must surely be one of the longest relationships of that sort in present-day publishing. He became my editor more than forty years ago.

There's no real accounting for that kind of longevity, but one thing that helped is that we got off to an exceptionally good start, not in commercial terms but in terms of Michael's involvement with my fiction.

The book we started out with, *Moving On*, is a book partly about graduate school, partly about rodeo, and partly about the indecision that is likely to afflict young marrieds, particularly those who belonged to what used to be called the Silent Generation.

As it happened, the young marrieds who populate *Moving On*, particularly my lachrymose heroine, Patsy Carpenter, were anything but silent. If Patsy wasn't chattering she was sobbing, a fact that didn't sit well with my women friends of the time—all of whom are still my women friends. These sprightly women had just discovered their not so latent feminism, and insisted, stoically, that they themselves never cried at all; or, if they did drip a tear now and then, it was in response to particularly atrocious behavior on the part of men. Since all the women I then knew cried practically all the time, I was at a loss as to how to answer this objection.

Michael Korda was then married to a Bennington girl named Casey, the first of his two wives. I never saw Casey Korda cry but I did hear her argue, and mainly with me, Michael having abdicated his role as Arguer-in-Chief as soon as I showed up in their apartment, which was on Sutton Place.

After a few minutes with Casey, whom I liked a lot, I began to understand why Michael liked *Moving On* so much. I'm glad that he did and that we got off to a good start—it helped steady us through the four decades of our relationship.

I don't see Michael very often, but when I do it's always a pleasure—one of the last times I had this pleasure took place in Amarillo, where Michael had gone to buy a secondhand Ferrari.

Knowledgeable as I am—or at least am said to be—about Texas, I had not realized until that day that Amarillo is one of the best places in

America to buy a secondhand Ferrari, and it's just the kind of thing that Michael Korda seems to know—it's the same knack that led him to find the costume he wore to our first dinner: neither like Nudies or like the dress of a real cowboy, what few there now are.

Though nominally retired from Simon and Schuster now, Michael, from his horse-rich enclave in Dutchess County, still edits me. The horses are for his second wife, Margaret, who, like President Obama, has spent some time in Kenya.

As an editor Michael normally eschews line editing and puts his formidable energies into seeing that the house gets behind the book, which, at the very least, means publishing it on time, which, so far, Simon and Schuster has always done. He's been just the right editor for me and I send him a salute, in part because I've just finished reading his excellent biography of General Eisenhower, called simply *Ike*.

I mentioned a while back that a large change in the thrust and tone of American letters occurred when *Howl* and *On the Road* were published, in the mid-Fifties. A bit of elaboration might be in order.

At the end of the Eighties, when, improbably, I became president of the PEN American Center, I saw a fair amount of Allen Ginsberg, and I liked him. Jack Kerouac I never met, and I regret that, because I think his one really good novel, *On the Road*, marked the real end of New Critical dominance of our literary culture. It was time for someone, Whitman-like, to burst out with a barbaric yarp, and Kerouac did it. I recently read the newly published "Scroll" edition and liked it a good deal better than I liked the tamer, shorter version that Viking tidied up and published in 1957. In this instance the writer knew better than the editors he worked with. I hope that someday the "Scroll" version will become the standard version—it's a far richer book.

Speaking of that time generally, I can still remember going to the news-stand that once operated on Commerce Street in Dallas, where I bought the famous "San Francisco Scene" issue of the *Evergreen Review*—issue # 2. Besides the text of *Howl*, the issue revealed to a largely startled readership that there were, on the West Coast, a number of poets and writers that few on the East Coast and not too many in the Midwest had ever heard of: people such as Robert Duncan, Kenneth Rexroth, Gary Snyder, Philip Lamantia, David Meltzer, and so on. Donald Allen soon published his important anthology *The New American Poetry*, and Kenneth Rexroth did a comprehensive piece for Theodore Solotaroff's *New American Review*, mentioning a great many writers I at once added to my reading list and sought in the bookshops.

Though not a poet myself—the two lyrics I published in the *Southwest Review* were my own only published poems, not counting a couple in the *Avesta*, the collegiate magazine I had mentioned earlier—I did recognize that knowing the work of these hitherto unknown poets was important. The cultural shift that they represented was significant. Good as Robert Lowell, Elizabeth Bishop, Anne Sexton, Delmore Schwartz, and others from the East Coast were, they were not, as it might have once seemed, the whole of the story.

In 1960, when I headed to Stanford to enjoy my Stegner Fellowship, I doubt I would have survived in a rigorously East Coast atmosphere. I was too gauche and to unread to have fit in. (Not that I particularly fit in with the West Coast poetry crowd, either. Except for David Meltzer, and, later, Allen Ginsberg, I never met any of the poets mentioned in the *Evergreen Review on The New American Poetry*.)

The one East Coast writer I was really interested in at the time was Norman Mailer, whom I was not to meet until I had moved to D.C. and opened the bookshop I was to run with Marcia Carter for so long. Once, in the heyday of Willie Morris's editorship of *Harper's*, my Texas friend

Larry L. King called and said Mailer was in town and would we like to have dinner? We did. Mailer was way across the table from me—so far that I scarcely exchanged two words with him. I did note that when we changed wines he chided the waiter for not bringing him a clean glass to do the tasting from. He also dismayed Marcia, who was seated near him, by telling her that she looked a little like Jack Carson, a comedian now not much remembered, except by Marcia.

In my years as president of PEN's American Center, I saw a good deal of Norman Mailer—he was always polite and helpful and he and his wife, Norris Church Mailer, who hailed from Little Rock, were gracious enough to give a dinner for me as the PEN drama was ending. He had been president of the same PEN himself, and mostly kept mum about his involvement with that organization. I had always admired very much the supra-journalistic work he did in the Sixties and Seventies—the *Armies of the Night* years.

At the farewell dinner he and Norris gave for me I was able to meet one of my idols, the gossip columnist Taki Theodoracopulos. I told him that I subscribed to *The Spectator*, his principal outlet, in three cities (D.C., Archer City, Tucson) just in order to read him. I've dropped two of the cities but I still subscribe to *The Spectator* and I still do so mainly to read Taki.

This, in its way, is a curious fact, since I have never met and probably never will meet most of the people Taki writes about. Why? I suppose because he is able to make a lot of rich strangers interesting. Since he's written his "High Life" column successfully for decades I'd say he has a gift.

In the years when the Mississippi writer and editor Willie Morris reigned supreme at *Harper's* magazine I met, simply by being in Washington, many of the New Journalists he nurtured. An old colleague of Willie's, the Texas writer Larry L. King, was probably the writer from this group whom I saw most often. Larry was from Midland-Odessa; after years of scraping by in D.C., sometimes by working on the Hill, sometimes by writing highly colorful pieces, mostly about Texas, Larry L. King finally struck it rich by writing a musical called *The Best Little Whorehouse in Texas*, a charming effort that is no doubt still playing in some theater somewhere.

I had met Willie Morris once or twice in Texas. Before rising to the editorial chair at *Harper's* he had first edited *The Texas Observer*, a gadfly liberal rag which is still in Austin and still gadflying.

When Marcia and I first opened the bookshop Willie was, I believe, involved with the witty, vivacious D.C. talk show hostess Barbara Howar, whose house was only one block from our bookshop.

Larry L. King, at some point I believe, succeeded Willie in Barbara's affection, although possibly a well-known Russian poet squeezed into the succession in Barbara's parlor for a time. What is certain is that, in Willie's eyes, the crude West Texan Larry L. King was far too vulgar a specimen to be trusted with this delicate Southern Lily, Barbara Howar. Legend has it that, after brooding about this violation for a while, from somewhere deep in his cups, he rose and attempted to strangle his former friend Larry L. King in Barbara's parlor. Larry L. King, seeing how things were, accepted a certain amount of abuse before rising up and punching Willie so hard that Willie fell out of the house, down some steps, and into 31st Street.

I was new to Washington when these fitful things happened. Barbara had managed to inspire Willie Morris to write a novel poetically entitled *The Last of the Southern Girls*, which was published about the same time Barbara Howar published her lively memoir *Laughing All the Way*, which no one in the Georgetown in crowd seemed to want to review. I soon reviewed the two books in one review, called "Wringing the Belle"—not my title but a good enough one.

I managed to say nice things about both books—or so I thought— but I believe Willie considered that I had not been nearly nice enough to either one. He expressed his umbrage by crossing the street every time he passed the bookshop. Then we got bookshops on both sides of 31st Street, presenting Willie with a tactical dilemma. When traffic permitted he chose the middle of the street; fortunately he soon ceased to be in Washington much and his duels with the Georgetown traffic blessedly occurred no more.

Many years later Willie Morris came into the bookshop with James Jones—the two had been touring Civil War battlefields. Willie was so drunk that he sank into a chair and did not utter a word, but James Jones was courteous, friendly, and very curious about the rare book world.

Barbara Howar eventually left Washington too. The last time I saw her she was doing her best to cheer up my then agent Irving Paul "Swifty" Lazar. Irving's beloved wife, Mary, had died a few months earlier and everyone who cared for Irving, and many did, tried to help him, but to no avail. He died about a year after Mary—of, among other things, gangrene, because he wouldn't give up his handmade English shoes. On the night I dined with them Barbara was driving for Irving, which would tax anyone's patience, anytime, since it was likely to bring down torrents of abuse as it did in this instance, but Barbara Howar mainly shrugged it off.

A caveat: I was never part of the Washington in crowd and cannot vouch for the veracity of Willie Morris's fight with Larry L. King, or, indeed, what I was told about that and many other legendary events.

I still think occasionally of James Jones, partly because I had always admired his fiction and also because he behaved so well with a seriously drunk Willie Morris on his hands. And I remember that the single most vicious letter I have ever read was the letter Hemingway wrote Scribners when they asked him to give a blurb to *From Here to Eternity*. It's there, in the *Selected Letters* for all to read, an example of a once great writer at his very worst. I doubt that he ever forgave Scribners for publishing James Jones in the first place. War, as Hemingway saw it, belonged to him.

Willie Morris, while editor of *Harper's*, found himself engaged in a battle of wills with the owners of the magazine—a battle having to do with budgets, policies, etc. As a countermove he sent in a letter of resignation, assuming that it would be rejected. It wasn't—his resignation dislodged Willie from the job that made him famous. He wrote a fine memoir called *North Toward Home*, and also a lovely book about his dog Skip. He died, I believe, in Oxford, Mississippi, not very far from Yazoo City, where he grew up.

I regret that the incidence of the review—which, like two others I wrote, was, despite what the authors felt, essentially favorable—kept me from knowing Willie Morris well. (The two others were Viva and Richard Ford. The latter finally relented but Viva, I fear, still thinks I gave a bad review to a book of hers I had actually praised.)

10

EXCEPT FOR THE members of the Stegner class itself I met few writers during my first year in the Bay Area. This was probably because so many Bay Area writers were poets, and poets have a tendency to stay home and work.

One novelist I did meet was Herbert Gold, who was then living in San Francisco. He was later to edit a good anthology of writings of the Fifties. Originally he hailed from Cleveland, I believe. He seemed to be a gentle, nonaggressive person who gave the impression of being somewhat out of touch, which is perhaps why his first novel is called *The Man Who Was Not with It*, a book once held to be a candidate for the first Beat novel, along with such forgotten artifacts as Nolan Miller's *Why I Am So Beat* and John Clellon Holmes's *Go*.

In my opinion none of the books which chronicled what might be called a Beat lifestyle were remotely as good as *On the Road*, which didn't mean their authors weren't quirky. Most of them are forgotten today but Herbert Gold has at least one fan: me. Somehow Herb had found out that I had written something in which there was an act of bestiality: specifically some local youths in Texas, having no other outlet, chose to have sex with a heifer. My first editor, John Leggett, had also heard about this, possibly from reading the manuscript of *The Last Picture Show*, in which the act of unnatural congress occurs.

John Leggett eventually turned down *The Last Picture Show*, though I doubt that the sex-with-the-heifer scene had much to do with his decision, which was probably based on weak sales of my first two books.

Such congress is, of course, common in rural areas the world over, although the late C. L. Sonnichsen, distinguished historian of the Southwest that he was, could not bring himself to accept this. He delivered himself of a searing polemic called *From Hopalong to Hud* in which he raged against the horrible smear I had delivered on decent American farm boys. He called what I called beastiality zoophilly, which, as I pointed out to him, is a term that came out of the anti-vivisection movement, a distinction to which Dr. Sonnichsen did not reply. Zoophilly has nothing to do with the habit farm boys cultivate of having sex with practically any animal they could catch.

Of course there are numerous examples in classical statuary of such trans-species sexual activity—the satyr and the goat for one, and Leda and the swan.

A final, slightly curious aspect of my Stanford year was that there was a poetry seminar running concurrently with the Stegner fiction seminar, and yet I never met even one Stanford poet—that is, I didn't at the time. Yvor Winters, whose students the poets were, evidently believed that no good could come of his poets meeting their equals in the fiction seminar. He may well have been right. Later I did meet one Stanford poet, Gus Blaisdell, who, for years, ran an excellent bookshop near the campus of the University of New Mexico, in Albuquerque.

Like most Stanford poets from this era, Gus was fanatically loyal to Yvor Winters. Gus unfortunately is now "late," as they say of the deceased in the delightful Botswana novels of Alexander McCall Smith.

Later I read Yvor Winters's criticism, and his poetry, and found both good. I didn't then learn of his complicated friendship with Hart Crane. It was to Winters, I believe, that Crane sent the first draft of *The Bridge*, which is a little like Eliot showing a draft of *The Wasteland* to Ezra Pound.

Although I wrote a decent piece about Janet Lewis, Winters's brilliant wife, for *The New York Review of Books*, I still feel that she is underrated, both as a novelist and a poet. When I drove up to her house in Los Gatos the name on the mailbox of the address I had was Arthur Yvor Winters.

I enjoyed my little time with Janet Lewis very much, and believe still that she was one of the great women of American letters. Her brilliant novella *The Wife of Martin Guerre* is one of the finest of American short fiction. When I spoke of it she said that when she wrote it she had been trying to write formula fiction for *Redbook*, to bring in a little money, and was having trouble with plots. Her husband gave her an old law book he had found—a book on evidence—out of which she got not only *Martin Guerre* but two other engaging historical novels, *The Trial of Soren Quist* and *The Ghost of Monsieur Scarron*.

Janet Lewis died a few months after my visit. I had heard somewhere that Nabokov was a friend and even sometimes helped her wash up after dinner. When I asked about this she smiled and said, "I wouldn't be surprised if he did."

11

WALLACE STEGNER WAS away from Stanford the year in which I held his fellowship. But he had not yet left when I arrived and was more friendly to me than was ever to be the case again. I told him I was book scouting and he kindly let me fill in some gaps in the holdings of the Jones Room—the Jones Room was the gracious comfortable library room next to the classroom where the actual seminars were held. It is, alas, no more.

Stegner soon left and Malcolm Cowley and, in the second semester, Frank O'Connor, took over. At the end of May 1961, the class ended and I went back to Texas. It was more than twenty-five years before I returned to the Stanford campus, although I had had another interlude in San Francisco in 1962.

My return to Stanford after a quarter of a century was to honor Wallace Stegner for his long service at the school. I added my voice to a chorus of praise. What I mainly had to praise him for myself was arranging for the Jones Room to buy some books from me.

The honors for Wallace Stegner of course involved dinners and parties and patrons, and it seemed to me, knowing him little, that Wallace Stegner was not entirely at ease with these proceedings.

Several years later there was a second round of honors, which I also attended, and it seemed to me that Mr. Stegner was, if possible, even less at ease with *these* proceedings, which were of the same nature as the first proceedings.

Sometime earlier I had given *Wolf Willow*, Stegner's autobiography, a very favorable review—it's a wonderful book, and when I saw him, he mentioned the review and thanked me for it.

It was, indeed, after reading *Wolf Willow* that I began to read Wallace Stegner in earnest. I started at the end of his fiction, *Crossing to Safety*, and then moved back to *Angle of Repose*, which won the Pulitzer Prize. These are both excellent novels, though, personally, I have a slight preference for *Crossing to Safety*.

I also much enjoyed a little book of his essays called *Where the Blue-bird Sings to the Lemonade Springs*. I read his important biography of the explorer-ethnographer John Wesley Powell (*Beyond the Hundredth Meridian*) and also his study of Mormonism, the faith he was born into. My respect for his body of work increased as I read.

Part of Stegner's unease with the series of honors he was offered was a deep disagreement with Stanford about the direction the writing program—which he had created and supported for many years—would take once he left. If there was a serious debate Wallace Stegner lost it. When I visited Stanford on the second surge of honors what had been the Stegner fiction seminar was being taught by Gilbert Sorrentino, a fine writer but not one Wallace Stegner can have been greatly sympathetic to.

To my shock my handlers simply dropped me into the fellowship fiction class one afternoon, leaving me embarrassed and almost speechless. Gilbert Sorrentino was perfectly courteous but he must have felt my arrival to be a most unwelcome intrusion—certainly his students did.

Academies breed feuds, a fact I had long since accepted. Wallace Stegner's final feud with Stanford, however it began, did not end happily for him. I heard that his papers, which had been on deposit at Stanford, were moved to Brigham Young.

*　　*　　*

Some years back the ever expanding Library of America called me one day and asked if I thought Wallace Stegner deserved inclusion in this prestigious assemblage of American literature. I said I thought he most certainly did, but when they asked if I would oblige them by editing a volume or two, I declined, mainly because I had not read much of Mr. Stegner's early fiction, of which there is a lot. I thought Wallace Stegner's son Page was best suited to undertake this task, but, so far, no Stegner volumes have appeared in the Library of America, which is a pity.

Once a mischief-maker sent me a copy of a letter from Stegner—a conservationist hero—to Senator Tim Wirth of Colorado. Mr. Stegner (I always called him that) said that I was a Texas romantic and that the famous revisionist Patricia Nelson Limerick would soon take care of me. I have never met Patricia Nelson Limerick but I have reviewed a book or two of hers and received a friendly response. Why she would be wanting to "take care" of me I cannot quite fathom, nor, I would imagine, can she, since she has more than once invited me to the famous Center of the American West at the University of Colorado in Boulder.

Wallace Stegner cracked, and then rejected, the Eastern establishment, more or less. He taught at Harvard, and enjoyed a long friendship with the once famous critic, historian, and newspaper man Bernard DeVoto. I don't think Stegner has had his due—he wrote seven or eight really good books, but it may be that his due will come later.

He died as the result of a car crash in New Mexico.

12

Meanwhile, what of my own literary life once the Stegner class ended and its participants drifted off to various faraway spots on the globe: Chris Koch back to Australia, Kesey (eventually) back to Oregon, Dave Godfrey to Canada, Gurney Norman and Jim Hall back to Kentucky, and Peter S. Beagle just down the road to Santa Cruz.

I myself got a job in Fort Worth, at TCU, teaching five classes of freshmen some version of English. It was by a long measure the hardest teaching job I ever held.

On the bright side that year I met John Graves, whose fine book *Goodbye to a River*, a lovely pastoral, had just come out. I also met probably the most extraordinary of John's students, Dave Hickey, of whom more later—though not much more. Dave, a brilliant writer, remains something of a mystery to himself and others.

My then wife, Jo, and I lived in a tiny house near the TCU campus, and, in March, our son, James, was born.

Rather to my surprise a well-dressed man from Paramount Studios showed up, took me to dinner, and said that my first novel, *Horseman, Pass By*, was going to be made into a movie, *Hud*, and, a little later in the year, sure enough it was.

Meanwhile, with the movie money burning a hole in our pockets, Jo,

James, and I moved to San Francisco for a spell, and then, at the beginning of 1963, settled in Austin.

By then the Hollywood money had burned its way through every pocket that we had—all $10,000 of it, which is nothing now but a very respectable sum then. Fortunately, once again, Rice came to my rescue. They needed a lecturer in English, someone they could hire year by year, for a while, so we moved back to Houston, accompanied, for a brief while, by Billy Lee Brammer, who was way down on his luck—never mind that his novel *The Gay Place* had made him famous or at least notorious.

Our home was a modest house on Quenby Road; Billy Lee, with the use of many blankets, made himself an air-conditioned cubicle in the garage.

At Rice I had only to teach two classes, and, even better, I could teach pretty much what I happened to be reading. As an academic experience my years at Rice as a lecturer were as good as it was ever to get.

While in Austin I had actually finished *Leaving Cheyenne* to my satisfaction and, fortunately, to John Leggett's satisfaction too. It's a *Jules et Jim*–like novel about a very long relationship between a rancher, his hired hand, and the woman they both love. I was very young and cannot have known much about long relationships when I wrote it, but still, it seemed to work and is the very favorite of many of my readers.

About this time too I began to get occasional magazine work.

Holiday Magazine asked me more or less to bisect Texas, from the Mexican to the New Mexican borders. Brownsville to Texline, that would be. I was supposed to stop and talk to people along the way, taking the measure of contemporary Texas, more or less. I drove the drive, but I made no attempt to talk the talk. What I did was invent a café called the Texas Moon and placed it in Harlingen, I believe. In the (invented) café two (invented) old men were speculating about the age of a piece of apricot pie—that was pretty much the best I could do when it came to feeling the pulse of the state, although I did, to give balance, make up an epically tasteless chicken-fried steak as served at an unnamed café in the Panhandle. Some residents of the Panhandle have never forgiven me for that piece of description, although probably at least one hundred thousand slabs of chicken-fried steak, no better and no worse than the one I describe, are consumed in the Panhandle of Texas every day.

In this short period I also attended an old fiddler's contest in East Texas, little knowing that my own son, James, would be participating in just such events at the very beginnings of his musical career.

13

In the summer of 1964 a family crisis erupted in Archer City. If the Pan-handle chicken-fried steak was no different from thousands of others, likewise my family crisis. All over the world family crises of just that nature happen, one after another, all the families allowing themselves to be taken completely by surprise by some of the most often repeated actions humans are capable of.

The effect of this crisis was to make me even more wary of Archer City than I already had been. Simply put, it's not a nice town. But the bright flare of crisis prompted me to write a bleak novel called *The Last Picture Show*, describing not the crisis but the culture that caused the crisis to erupt in the way that it did. That book, written in three weeks, eventually, over forty-five years, became a quintet, the fifth volume of which, *Rhino Ranch*, has recently appeared.

Like *Horseman, Pass By*, *The Last Picture Show* was also snapped up by the movies, Columbia Studios securing it very quickly, though it did not, like the earlier book, achieve rapid passage to the screen—in this case there was no star raring to do it. It took about seven years to find its way to the screen. A first script was done, not by me, giving this bleak tale a happy ending. Then it came loose from the first option and got made with a cast of small names—but the complicated making of *The Last Picture Show* is a story for the third Hollywood volume of these memoirs.

From a technical, writerly point of view, the interesting thing about *The Last Picture Show* is literally the book's point of view. I had written two novels told in the first person (and was, in time, to write several more). But I felt the time had come to stretch a little, which meant trying to write something in the third person. The first person came easily for me—I imagine it comes easy for most of those who employ it. So easy was it for me that, in fact, I wrote the first draft of *Picture Show* in the old, familiar first person and then laboriously translated it into third.

Once I learned how to do the third person I have mostly stuck with it, only rarely—as in *Somebody's Darling*, retreating to first.

Probably that one aspect of fiction—point of view—has provoked more critical prose than any other element. Billions of words have been spoken about it in zillions of the creative writing classes that dot the academic globe. The reason the first person is so seductive, as a point of view, is who *shows* the reader what seems to be going on. Only make them See! Conrad famously said, when asked about his guiding principles as a future writer. I believe the one gift I had that led me to a career in fiction was the ability to make up characters that readers connect with. My characters move them, which is also why those same characters move them when they meet them on the screen.

14

DESPITE THE RIGORS of my five-class year at TCU, one or two good things happened. I met, as reported, the fine writer John Graves, and his then student, the brilliant Dave Hickey.

But, thanks to the five classes, meeting them was about all I had time to do—then our paths parted and I've never known either of them well.

John Graves is a solitary-seeming man, although he has a wife and two grown daughters. Early on he produced *Goodbye to a River*, his enduring masterpiece. John is possessed of an urbane, even European sensibility—he lived in Spain for a while, I believe. He came home because a section of the Brazos River he had long canoed and loved was due to be dammed. With a canoe and a puppy he ran it one last time, paddling, in effect, through the history of that part of the world.

Though written in supple, unornamented prose, *Goodbye to a River* is essentially a lyric elegy, to a place and a way of life John cared deeply about.

I heard that John had ambitions to be a fiction writer, and he has written a few remarkable stories, notably one called "The Last Running." But his novels, if they exist, were not well received in the East.

I don't know how long John Graves kept his connection with TCU. He built himself a stone house near the Brazos and lives there still. He wrote a good account of his life amid the rocks and gullies, called *Hard Scrabble*, a title that says a lot.

Jane Graves, John's mate, is a Long Island lady whose affection for the hardscrabble life is not always evident. She worked for a good many years as a buyer for Neiman Marcus in Dallas—a considerable distance from the stone house near the Brazos. Since her commute home often involved driving after dark, she invented an inflatable companion to help her get through the shit-kickers and other dangers.

John's favorite stretch of the Brazos is now the John Graves Memorial River, I believe, though both the man and the river still survive.

John, as a writer, has always kept his hand in, doing many introductions and forewords to books he likes. The last writing I have seen by him is a series on the Texas rivers, the ones that have meant most to him. These are being done for the Park Service magazine; I hope they will be a collection, for they all bear his distinctive stamp.

Some years ago I had a little Center in Archer City; there were writing classes in the summer, and acting classes for awhile; but, best of all, we got to give Life Achievement to deserving writers and actors. We quickly gave John one and I think he was pleased. I am always happy to come about John's work, wherever I find it. Every sentence he's written is readable.

My Center didn't last very long, but we did perhaps nudge a few students into fruitful paths. The Center itself ultimately failed, but not before causing some change in Archer City, which has now become a sort of seminar town. Twice or more a year groups of students come from afar, and spend a week or two pondering point of view and the other great verities.

The locals, as near as I can tell, are as indifferent to the students as they are to my bookshops—four large buildings crammed with books—or anything else that is not strictly local. You'd think the bookshops would qualify, since they take up most of downtown—but the books in them are not local and that's enough for most of the citizens of Archer City.

15

I WOULD BE skimping indeed if I ended my account of my time in Cow Town, as Fort Worth is still sometimes called, without expanding a little on my few fruitful glimpses of the protean Dave Hickey, now at last officially certified as a genius by the MacArthur Foundation of Chicago.

As long as I've known Dave I still am not sure what best to call him: writer, curator, art writer, editor (of *Art in America*), gallery owner, and the author of the best sentence ever to appear in *The Texas Observer* (I quote from long memory): "Even if one succeeds in making a silk purse of a sow's ear, there remains the problem of what to do with a one-eared sow."

Among the things Dave Hickey has done are:

A. Run, with his first wife, a gallery in Austin.

B. Edited a magazine in New York.

C. Written country songs in Nashville, including a notable one about Oscar Wilde and Billy the Kid.

D. Written a brilliant book of short stories.

E. Written several books about art, one of which soars as far above my head as calculus.

F. Curated a famous exhibit in Santa Fe.

G. Inhabited my ranch house for a time, just before his star rose.

H. Now teaches at the University of Nevada in Las Vegas.

Months after Dave's fortunes had risen I happened to be inhabiting the ranch house myself. I was, in fact, in the bathtub reading when I heard the front door open. Whoever entered—a cowboy, I assumed—came down the hall and turned out to be Dave.

"Oh, sorry," he said. "I just dropped in to borrow this volume of Coleridge's letters."

I haven't seen Dave Hickey since, but I do expect to see him eventually, probably in similar circumstances. I included his great story "The Closed Season" in a volume of stories from, more or less, the present-day West. The book is called *Still Wild*.

16

MY FIRST THREE novels, *Horseman, Pass By, Leaving Cheyenne,* and *The Last Picture Show,* felt, as I wrote them, quite unconnected to one another. I wasn't then used to thinking thematically. When I got a little distance from the three books I realized that they represented a kind of Exodus cycle—the exodus being the move country kids all over Texas were making in the Fifties—in droves the country kids were leaving the emptiness and bleakness of small-town life for the burgeoning cities and their ever advancing suburbs. And it was the kids with the most energy and the best brains who were leaving first.

At the end of *Horseman,* for example, Lonnie leaves the ranch. In *Leaving Cheyenne* Molly's cruel gay son has already left. In *Picture Show,* Duane leaves to serve in Korea, though, in time, he returns to Thalia and lives the rest of his life there.

Exodus, in my view, makes a great theme: the dying of the old, rural, agrarian culture, which was the only culture Texas really had until, in the Forties, the cities finally began to fill out.

My task, at least as I finally came to understand it, was to dramatize this exodus from both sides: first the rural, then the urban. The first three novels, consequently, showed the country kids leaving. The second three: *Moving On, All My Friends Are Going to Be Strangers,* and *Terms of Endearment,* all, or nearly all, set in Houston, dealt with new, or fairly new, urbanites. The best of the lot, *Terms of Endearment,* more or less completed my Exodus cycle.

17

THERE WAS, HOWEVER, a book that fell between, and that was my first book of essays, *In a Narrow Grave*. I had done a fair amount of spot journalism by this time, enough for a book, maybe. But when I offered this prospective book to Simon and Schuster they blanched and turned away. (A little later they reprinted it.)

Fortunately, about that time, I met Bill and Sally Wittliff, who ran a very classy regional publishing company called the Encino Press out of their home in Austin. Bill had already distinguished himself as a book designer and would, a little later, distinguish himself even more as a screenwriter-producer, and, maybe best of all, a photographer.

My small accumulation of essays, augmented by a long piece about my family and one or two others, gave Bill and Sally something to publish that looked at least a little way beyond the region. The Encino Press went on to publish about one hundred titles, and the one that got them in most trouble with the local literary establishment was *In a Narrow Grave*, mainly because I wrote an essay about the work of the hitherto unassailable idols trio: Roy Bedichek, Walter Prescott Webb, and, of course, J. Frank Dobie. I was not unkind to any of these writers, all of whom I respected in differing degrees. But I did point out that their writings were not entirely without flaw, which was heresy in Texas at that time.

In a Narrow Grave was in effect a kind of summing up of what I had observed during the passing of the rural way: the way of my father and mother and their people. It also happened to be the best-designed book I will ever have. Bill Wittliff was reaching his peak as a book designer just about then.

18

In the late Sixties I became entangled in the long novel that eventually became *Moving On*, a title supplied by Casey Korda. I began the book at Rice and finished it in the small town of Waterford, Virginia, not far from the Blue Ridge Mountains and the Potomac River.

Moving On was not the Great American Novel but for a time I thought it was. The only person to share my opinion was my new editor, Michael Korda. By the time I finished it, in 1969, I had a good deal of narrative momentum going. I felt something like Hemingway mentioned feeling in *A Moveable Feast*, when, in Spain, he wrote two stories in one day and was being prodded by a cheeky waiter to write a third. What Hemingway, in that regard, called Juice I call narrative momentum. I was on a kind of fatigue high, which I thought I could probably sustain long enough to write a good short book. No more baggy monsters—just a good short book, I felt.

Thus I sailed into *All My Friends* . . . which I wrote in about five weeks. The book was then and probably still remains the best entry point to my fiction, mainly because I was too tired to feel in the least self-conscious. I just spewed it out, and never, until now, looked back. *All My Friends* still, in my view, reads well.

All My Friends has not been as lucky with Hollywood as some of my other books have but it's certainly not for lack of interest. It has been scripted about a dozen times. Musicians, particularly, seem to like it. James Taylor had it under option for a while, as did the Eagles. Robert De Niro in his youth came down to D.C. to talk with me about it, and I received, one night, an enigmatic call from Mike Nichols, asking why, if he was getting so much pussy, my hero Danny Deck killed himself?

Danny Deck *doesn't* kill himself, actually, but Mr. Nichols and others can be forgiven for thinking so, since he's in the middle of the Rio Grande, in a distressed condition, when the novel ends.

Many years later I put to rest the vexed question of Danny Deck's survival by writing a novel called *Some Can Whistle*, in which Danny Deck, TV producer, is very much alive.

He also finds T.R., the daughter he lost at the end of *All My Friends*.

19

In the early Seventies, when I was trying, with my partner, Marcia Carter, to establish a rare bookshop in Washington, D.C., Hollywood shoved its way into my life again—since then, fortunately for me, it never really left.

The young director Peter Bogdanovich had a large success with the movie version of *The Last Picture Show*; he followed up this triumph with two more very successful films, *What's Up, Doc?* and *Paper Moon.* Peter Bogdanovich was, though he didn't know it, riding higher than he has yet to ride again. He divorced Polly Platt, his production designer wife, and fell in love with Cybill Shepherd, whom he was determined to make into a star—indeed, into a big star.

In the fullness of time Cybill Shepherd made herself into a big star, thanks to a TV series called *Moonlighting*, which also raised the fortunes of Bruce Willis, her co-star.

As for Peter Bogdanovich, his subsequent plans mostly did not quite gel. He had always wanted to make "Daisy Miller," the famous Henry James short story, and his three hits gave him the power to make most anything he wanted to, though it didn't mean he would necessarily make it well.

In the story, Daisy's obnoxious brother, Randolph, is eleven years old, just the age of my son, James, who got the part of Randolph without ever seeking it. The filming was done in Rome and Switzerland, where neither James nor I had ever been.

James was up for this adventure, so off to Rome we went. I had begun *Terms of Endearment*, the third volume in what would eventually be the Houston (or, if you prefer, *Terms*) tetralogy. Since I was assured that there were plenty of typewriters in Italy, I did not take one with me.

In fact there *were* an abundance of typewriters in Italy, but they had a rather different keyboard than what I was used to on my old Royal. We stayed at the Hilton and I spent most of my days pecking away at my story on an odd machine, in which the Z appeared where I had been used to finding an A, or possibly the E.

Later, when we finished in Rome and continued on to Switzerland, I discovered that I had yet another European keyboard to contend with. The differences were minor, but, to a creature of habit such as myself they were more than a little vexing.

James was mainly on the set all day, much pampered by the stout Italian ladies who got him dressed.

Because of the two typewriters the first draft of *Terms of Endearment* is a crazy quilt of As and Zs that seem really out of place.

In Switzerland we stayed at the Trois Couronnes, the fine hotel in Vevey, where, as it happened, Henry James had written (or at least conceived) the story.

Just as the crew was setting up for James McMurtry's final shot the fog settled over Lake Geneva; it didn't lift for almost three weeks. The hot chocolate was excellent—Nestlé's nestled nearby—but the fishing was about all that was keeping James McMurtry from terminal boredom— that and the futz ball games that he played more or less nightly with the crew—among whom was the now prominent producer Frank Marshall.

There was a small lending library just below the hotel, the Librairie

Payot, stocked mainly with English books of the sort that might appeal to genteel English ladies as they lived out their lives in Swiss luxury.

Back in Washington, where I had not been for a while, my partner, Marcia Carter, was growing alarmed by the rapid thinning out of our shelves. So alarmed was she that I *bought* the lending stock of the Librairie Payot and shipped it forthwith to Washington.

I was reminded of this long-ago transaction just last week, when I pulled a book off the shelf in Tucson and noticed the small neat book label of the Librairie Payot. A book I bought, probably in 1973, had come home to me again.

20

In 1969, when James and I moved to the East Coast, we entered a culture that was very different from the one we left in Texas. The (Texas-born) writer Katherine Anne Porter said somewhere that she wanted to live either in the country or in a capital, and she chose the capital for the last years of her life. She lived in a Maryland suburb of D.C. and, I am told, ordered her coffin several years before her death, using it as a coffee table first.

By the time we got well set up in northern Virginia, with the family of Sam, Eleanor, and Clayton Adams as our neighbors and best friends, I was in the throes of a kind of work trauma that probably afflicts most writers who write prolifically: I had ceased to like my own prose. I had, by then, written six books and was nearly finished with a seventh. Thanks to the two movies made from my work I had some credibility, but not much.

My own feeling was that my fiction had somehow lost all freshness. I knew that fallow periods were normal in the literary life, but still, I seemed unable to take my own in stride.

Another factor is that for ten years I had been writing about Emma Horton, a character I had come to love; but now Emma was dead. Characters who have long been with you become your friends. When I put a final period on Emma and her family, I lost presences that had been in my life for a long time. In some way I had leaned on them, but that was over. They were gone!

Fortunately I had the bookshop to absorb my energies. I never, even during the worst of times, exactly had writer's block—I still wrote my five pages every day. It was just that I no longer *liked* the five pages—at least not consistently. In fact I *disliked* them, sentence by sentence, as the sentences came out of the machine.

I am sure many writers, when in mid-career, experience these same feelings. You, the writer, will have done enough good work to have acquired some reputation, and yet you haven't done enough for it to be time to break the pencil (Faulkner's phrase), even if you could afford to financially, which I can't and never could have.

Although I think the last sixty pages of *Terms of Endearment* are among the very best pages I have written, it was while I was writing them that I began to sour on my own work. The minute I finished that book I fell into a literary gloom that lasted from 1975 until 1983, when the miracle of *The Desert Rose* snapped me out of it. In those years I produced what I consider to be two of my weakest books, *Somebody's Darling* and *Cadillac Jack*.

Somebody's Darling was my first attempt to deal with Hollywood in my fiction, and has very few fans, although one of the few happens to be my son, which heartens me a good deal.

Cadillac Jack doesn't have that many fans either, although John Mellencamp is one positive reader for whom I have great respect.

The unexpected arrival of *The Desert Rose* is a complex miracle, the story of which is best saved for my Hollywood memoir, which should follow close on the heels of this one.

21

If even tiny Archer City can attract three writing conferences a year, there must be hundreds or even thousands of such conferences scattered across this great land. Perhaps they are all, to some degree, children of Breadloaf, though maybe the writer's conference goes back even beyond Frost. The history of such conferences has not yet been written, but, when it is, I think the singular writer's conference organized in the summer of 1970, at Hollins College near Roanoke, Virginia, deserves at least a full chapter.

The organizers of this conference were the late novelist George Garrett and R. H. W. Dillard, the poet and for a time the husband of Annie Dillard, of *Pilgrim at Tinker Creek* fame, then a young woman who could hold her own at Ping-Pong, a game I once dominated in the writer's conference world, having picked it up from Hungarian jet pilots and Chinese mathematicians at Rice.

In the late Sixties and Seventies George Garrett was probably the most ubiquitous of the various writers who worked the high end of the university creative writing scene. I met George at Rice, from which he went on to Princeton and half a dozen other schools, never staying long at any one place but, as it were, covering the map. (After the debacle he helped create at Hollins, George became even more ubiquitous. The word on campus was that George and Richard Dillard had made themselves personally responsible for any loss the school might suffer; the loss, when totaled, was in the neighborhood of $95,000—the necessity to pay it off made George Garrett, for a time, the Henry Kissinger of shuttle academia, hustling for a year or two between several schools at once.) But what I report here is gossip-based and may not be true.

However, I'm getting ahead.

George Garrett wasn't blind, like James Thurber, but his preferred method of communication was the long letter, handwritten in a loping scrawl—a letter from George ran twenty-five to thirty pages, as a rule.

Sometime in 1970 I received one of these letters from George. It weighed slightly less than a bale of hay. It was not an easy letter to follow but the gist, as I interpreted it, was that I was being offered $10,000 to teach two courses at Hollins in the summer, for two weeks each. One course would be fiction, the other film—or, more specifically, the Western film, on which I was wrongly judged to be an expert.

If I wanted to do only one course the money would be halved. If I chose to teach the Western I could not only have my pick of films, I could also have my pick of times, since there would be a twenty-four-hour projection service.

It seemed, though odd, a curriculum made in heaven. Though I could certainly put the $10,000 to good use, I think it was the quirk of the round-the-clock projection that really appealed to me most.

And, it was all handy. I lived only about three hours up the road from Hollins. I accepted the two-course option—I would have been a fool not to. (I was not the only writer to think this way.)

Most of the various writer's conferences that I've attended involved lots of drinking and as much infidelity as the participants can squeeze in. The epic conference at Hollins in the summer of 1970 didn't vary from that model—it's just that there were more people involved than you usually find at such gatherings.

Looking back on it, what surprises me is that the Hollins conference of 1970 didn't produce a spate of novels, poems, tattle, memoirs, short stories, and the like. I have no doubt that everyone who was there had themselves received multi-page letters from George, promising money and possibly other inducements as well.

The headliners of this conference were, I guess, Ralph Ellison and James Dickey. Ellison did come, but briefly—I missed him entirely—but James Dickey was very much in evidence. Most of the time he sat on the porch of the big house, playing his guitar. He had arrived in the company of a nice middle-aged woman, said to be a former stripper whose stage name was the Miami Hurricane.

Whatever her name or her abilities, James Dickey, faced with a campus full of nubile young rich girls, very soon abandoned the Miami Hurricane, who proceeded to have a very miserable time. Many husbands less obnoxious than James Dickey were soon bent on fresh fields and pastures new.

I wish I had kept a definitive list of all the writers who attended the Hollins conference of 1970, but I didn't. Here, culled from a leaky memory, are the ones I still remember:

Ralph Ellison
James Dickey
Richard Wilbur (usually to be found on the tennis courts)
George Garrett
Richard Dillard
Annie Dillard
James Tate
Lee Smith

Peter Taylor
David Slavitt
Michael Mewshaw
Margaret Randall
John Little

The last named, John Little, became a first-rate organizer of writer's conferences himself; most of his were held in February in his power base at the University of North Dakota, in Grand Forks. These were attended mainly by the hardy souls that are confident enough of their weather skills to venture out in midwinter.

In the second week of the Hollins Conference I think many of us had begun to feel that one week of blathering about literature would have been enough. Ditto about film, of which there turned out to be very little.

My celebrated course on the Western, held at the moderate hour of one A.M., drew only a sprinkling of students, none of whom were very interested in the Westerns I chose to show them—the one exception was the brilliant Brazilian film *Antonio das Mortes*, which, among other virtues, had one of the longest shootouts in all cinema. Yet the kids watched it—on the screen pigs and chickens kept getting in the way of the fighting. As for the rest of world cinema my picks were cautious, or at least that's how I remember them. I believe I showed a Budd Boetticher or two, but can't now remember which.

I really liked George Garrett's wife, Susan. As the conference progressed from time to time she and I compared notes. Early in the second week Susan gave me some succinct advice, which was to invent an excuse, get my money, and leave.

The money, she assured me, was about to run out.

Within an hour I had my money and was gone. I'm not sure I bothered with an excuse, and I'm not sure anyone would have cared if I had. I was probably just off the campus when the roof began to cave in.

About this time, the gossips said, George Garrett became infautuated with a young female writer, of which there were several at the conference. He may/may not have promised this young lady publication in a well-known quarterly in exchange for certain erotic favors. Whether he did or didn't, Susan Garrett conceived a dislike for the young woman and prepared a revenge of some ingenuity: she purchased a large fish, let it age for a few days, and then placed it in the young woman's bed. True/not true I don't know, but I have certainly known women who would happily stoop to such an act.

The last time I saw George Garrett, who is now "late" in the Botswanian sense, he was in his football lineman stance, in a cornfield near Grand Forks, North Dakota, at midnight in February. He and I had been lured into the chill by the chance to bump heads with various celebrities: the late John Houseman, Joan Tewkesbury (screenwriter of *Nashville*), and Marcel Ophuls, director of *The Sorrow and the Pity*. Leslie Marmon Silko was there—we seemed to be the only writers present that year and, in fact, by then Leslie herself had made a film.

The fact that John Little (now "late" himself) could attract such talents to a freezing place comes down, as usual, to one thing: money.

22

I MENTIONED EARLIER that money has seldom played a decisive part in my career decisions, but there were exceptions, of course, and one particular period proved to be an exception.

At the beginning of the Eighties I was feeling bad about my prose. It wasn't any one thing—it was more like *everything*.

The one bright spot, financially, was that I had just sold *Cadillac Jack*, for, I believe, a $25,000 advance, a sum I assumed would easily pay my income tax.

A few minutes with my tax accountant revealed, to my horror, that I had been far too optimistic, not about what I had earned but about what I owed. It was $50,000, not half that amount.

It was the beginning of March, forty-five days to Armageddon, when I made this discovery.

What to do? (Many a writer, of course, has had to ask him- or herself that very question. Think Dostoyevsky!)

What I did was write, in twenty-two days, *The Desert Rose*, a book that seemed to flow out of me as rapidly as I could type. *The Desert Rose* was supposed to have been a screenplay, but, to my intense relief, it came out a novel. I had hardly written a sentence I liked for eight years: to actually enjoy my own prose again was a big, big deal.

My literary agent for the first thirty years of my career was Dorothea Oppenheimer, a beautiful European who acquired me as a client in 1960 and remained my agent until her death from pancreatic cancer three decades later. Though she lived to read *Lonesome Dove*, she didn't live to see it win a Pulitzer Prize for fiction, and to rise a fair ways on the *New York Times* bestseller list.

As Dorothea began to fail, my next agent, Irving Paul "Swifty" Lazar, began to quietly take over some of Dorothea's chores—indeed it was Irving's being so nice to Dorothea at her painful end that persuaded me to make him my agent when she died.

23

THE WILD SUCCESS of the film of *The Last Picture Show*—Jack Kroll of *Newsweek* said it might be the best American film since *Citizen Kane*—changed many lives, but, most especially, it changed the life of Peter Bogdanovich, his then wife, Polly Platt, and Cybill Shepherd—not to mention the lives of the two Bogdanovich children, Antonio and Alexandra.

Ever since I've known Peter Bogdanovich, and I've known him going on four decades, he has been talking about making a Western. He has yet to make one—Westerns are hard to finance now—but perhaps he'll get lucky and make one yet.

Of course the success of *Picture Show* gave Peter Bogdanovich immediate power: he could, for a time, have made pretty much any picture he wanted to make. But, just then, he had no Western to make.

Cybill Shepherd, as it happened, *did* have a movie to make: Elaine May had cast her in *The Heartbreak Kid,* much of which was filmed in Miami. Peter accompanied her but, as it turned out, didn't have much to do. He invited me down to wrestle with the question of finding, or inventing, a makable Western. Peter wanted this unmade and uninvented Western to star John Wayne, James Stewart, and Henry Fonda. The film, if it got made, would serve as a kind of homage to three men who had achieved much in the Western film. It would, in a way, he hoped, kind of top their achievements off.

The actors themselves, as might have been expected, didn't go for this, even after I had coughed up a pretty workable script. What we had planned was a sort of last adventure, after which they would be over, as would the Old West.

The three actors, though, saw no reason for the Old West to end, and, if for some reason it did *end* they wanted the last adventure to be a wild success, not a dim moral victory of the sort we had planned for them.

This project Peter and I proposed neither ripened nor died on the vine: it just circulated for a decade—this, frankly, is what most scripts do, until the day comes when they either get made or don't circulate anymore.

James Stewart and Henry Fonda, needing work, a factor that is decisive for most actors when it comes to script selection, eventually, if reluctantly, came aboard, but not so Wayne, who had plenty of work. He passed, and no one can be sure why. Maybe he didn't like it that James Stewart got to play the more poetic character. Maybe he didn't like Peter, or the script, or because he was tired of playing the competent grump yet one more time.

The project was with Warner Bros., and stayed there, neither quite alive nor quite dead. There were several other actors who might have played the role Wayne turned down: Burt Lancaster, Gregory Peck, but, so far as I know, it wasn't offered to them. Peter Bogdanovich went on to direct *What's Up, Doc?*, and *Paper Moon*, then a series of disasters—but I'll save that for my Hollywood book.

I was in need of money, and also, though I might not have been able to recognize it, in need of a theme. The Exodus cycle was finished. It had taken several more novels to exhaust the Exodus theme, but exhausted it was; I had to find somewhere else to go, and where turned out to be behind me, to an earlier time in the West when settlers like my grandparents were just coming to the West and building the little communities and homesteads that their grandchildren would abandon fifty years later.

I am, of course, from a ranching background. A few of my older uncles had done some modest trail driving. The trail drives and the myth of the cowboy which rose out of them were in the scope of my family memory. A trail driving novel might work—in fact I had already written a few fragments about cowboys and Texas Rangers—they were inconsequential but offered a place to start.

When I decided to do a three-book memoir I assumed that the line between subjects would be easy to draw: *Books* would be about my life as a rare bookman, *Literary Life* about my career as a writer, and *Hollywood* about, obviously, Hollywood.

In practice I soon found that I could not keep much of a fence between the subjects at all; and, really, I have kept almost none between my literary life and my Hollywood life. It all simply bleeds together. My work as a screenwriter-for-hire has gone a long way toward financing my book business, and the fact that several of my novels have been made into movies has made it easier to sell the next novel, of which there are now twenty-nine.

When I was writing *Horseman, Pass By* I did not for one moment look ahead to *Hud*, the film made from it. But, partly because *Hud* was so successful, book after book was optioned for the movies—some got made well, some got made poorly, and some didn't get made at all, but there were still the option checks, which didn't bounce.

As with *Hud*, so with *The Last Picture Show*. When I started writing it I had no idea that seven years later Peter Bogdanovich and Polly Platt would show up to start making it into a movie.

The present volume, *Literary Life*, is mainly about how the books came to me, but since many of them passed right through me and became movies, it is not possible to keep all the Hollywood stuff out of what was meant to be the literary volume. I can at least hold the stories of some of the more than fifty scripts of mine that did *not* become movies until we leave literary events and move along to Hollywood.

24

Lonesome Dove, of all my novels, was, by a large measure, the most difficult to finish. The first early gropings, in which an author could be seen trying to find a subject, were, when I looked at them carefully, not much help either, and neither was the earlier script written with Peter Bogdanovich, being, as I have already stated, about a different theme.

All I understood about *Lonesome Dove* then was that it would have to be long. Some cowboys would be driving a large trail herd all the way from Texas to Montana—South Texas to northern Montana, to be precise. (It had to be northern Montana because of the book that inspired it, the cowboy-rancher Teddy Blue Abbott's *We Pointed Them North*.) Teddy Blue, when, after some wild years, settled down, established a ranch on the Milk River, which is not far from Canada.

The drive, then, would be from the Rio Grande to the Milk: that, at first, was all I knew.

Add to initial ignorance about the story—which is common enough—I also had the more serious drawback of not having a satisfactory title.

In time, despite these drawbacks, and only rather lukewarm interest, I wrote two partial drafts of *Lonesome Dove*, leaving off just shy of five hundred pages each time.

I wrote a draft and stopped it to write *Cadillac Jack*; I wrote another and stopped it to write *The Desert Rose*.

I then went back to the inchoate mass of pages having to do with the two aging Texas Rangers and their friends. I rewrote what I could find of the earlier drafts and inched up toward five hundred pages again.

Then I got a break, a gift from the Muse if there ever was one.

There is a fine steakhouse called the Ranchman's, in a tiny town called Ponder, Texas, near Denton and not far from Fort Worth. I have eaten at the Ranchman's with some regularity for about fifty-five years. It was summer and I happened to be in the neighborhood, so I ate there again, emerging, well fed, at about dusk.

A few miles south of Ponder, with the lights of Fort Worth just ahead, I happened to notice an old church bus parked beside the road, and on its side was written: Lonesome Dove Baptist Church.

If ever I had an epiphany it was at that moment: I had, at last, found a title for the trail driving book.

I promptly went home and—somewhat anticlimactically—finished the book.

Why did I so instantaneously conclude that *Lonesome Dove* was my title?

I think it is because there is a kind of lonesome dove in the story, Captain Call's unacknowledged son, Newt.

And why wouldn't Captain Call, a man known for his high ethical standards, acknowledge the son that everyone knew was his; he had fathered Newt on a whore named Maggie, who died when Newt was young. The Ranger troop raises Newt, with Captain Woodrow Call taking only a minimal part.

I wrote the book and saw it become acclaimed, more so—indeed, *much more so*—than any of my other twenty-eight fictions.

Mainly through the excellent work of Bill Wittliff, my former publisher, mentioned earlier, *Lonesome Dove* was made into a miniseries, and released on CBS in 1989.

I went on to write three more novels about the same people: *Streets of Laredo, Dead Man's Walk,* and *Comanche Moon,* all of which were made into miniseries with very varying degrees of success. Two of these were made for CBS, the third for ABC.

Comanche Moon, the last of the quartet to reach the (small) screen, was aired in 2007. As I watched it with my writing partner, Diana Ossana, who co-wrote and co-produced it, I pondered, again, the question that tugged at me from the start: why wouldn't Captain Call acknowledge his son?

I still don't really know, and the fact that I don't has made me slightly suspicious of that long endeavor and its famous result.

25

THE DAY I found out that *Lonesome Dove* had been awarded the Pulitzer Prize, I happened to be lecturing at a small college in Uvalde, Texas. I think I may have been the first writer to speak in Uvalde, home of John Nance Garner, Roosevelt's outspoken vice president (for a while) who remarked famously that the vice presidency "wasn't worth a bootfull of warm spit." (There are variant versions, of course.)

Because they had never had a speaker before, the college in Uvalde wanted to be sure and get its money's worth, and they did. It was during my half-hour lunch break that I learned about the Pulitzer, a prize about which the writer William H. Gass has some pithy things to say.

James was living in San Antonio at the time—Uvalde was not far so he came over to help me celebrate, a doomed effort since I was dead tired from all day lecturing and had to drive to Austin, which *was* pretty far, to appear on a panel at the LBJ Library in the morning—a confab at which the then mayor of San Antonio, Henry Cisneros, brusquely insulted me.

As I was preparing to leave Uvalde I noticed the marquee of the Holiday Inn where I had been staying. When I arrived it read "Welcome to Larry McMurtry, Author of *Terms of Endearment*." By the next afternoon, despite a bunch of reporters showing up to interview me, the marquee had already been changed. Now it read: Catfish Special, $3.99.

Sic Transit Gloria DeHaven, as the fine Texas writer Edwin "Bud" Shrake once observed.

26

Lonesome Dove WAS my tenth novel, eleventh book. I had been publishing books from the early Sixties to the mid-Eighties before producing a book that came close to selling five thousand copies, a feat nearly achieved by *All My Friends*, which came out just in time to profit from the flare of interest produced by the popularity of *Picture Show*.

My lack of rising sales might have been easier for Simon and Schuster to tolerate if I had, along the way, been producing exceptional reviews, but, in the main, I attracted no reviews. After ten books I got a few paragraphs in *Newsweek*, and *The New York Times*, in their wisdom, sent *Leaving Cheyenne* to their Wyoming reviewer, although it plainly states that it's not about Wyoming.

The lack of interest in my books continues to this day. The single review of any interest and intelligence was written by Tad Friend and appeared in *The New York Review of Books*, a paper for which I was by then writing regularly.

The latest novel or story collection from Joyce Carol Oates will get more sharp reviewing attention than I can get, say, for my four-volume *Berrybender Narratives*, a not bad tetralogy.

Should I be bitter about the literary establishment's long disinterest in me? I shouldn't, and mostly I'm not, though I do admit to the occasional moment of irritation. Any writer with much self-respect would feel a twinge of annoyance at the inequalities of the critical marketplace. One should always keep a grain, or perhaps a pinch, of salt handy for these moments, while remembering the great axiom of John Maynard Keynes: "In the long run we'll all be dead." He was talking about economic policy when he said it but it applies equally well, it seems to me, to all policies.

As for literary opinion, as it applies to contemporary writers, I am much more willing to accept the judgment of time than I am the judgment of any literati. Time will sort us out, determine who was really good from who was mediocre.

This does not mean that I think I'm very likely to make the high-end cut. Little of my work in fiction is pedestrian, but, on the other hand, none of it is really great. Maybe it will seem better to readers fifty years from now than it does to me today. In either case I'll be with John Maynard Keynes and won't have to worry the question.

27

THE PUBLIC SUCCESS of *Lonesome Dove* did not, at the time, seem like a watershed event. Any long book, once finished, is likely to leave its author feeling a little slack. I wrote the last sentence and felt a little slack. In any case it was a year yet to publication, and even longer before it earned (if that's the word) its Pulitzer, and even longer still before the miniseries appeared and it rocketed to real fame, the kind that only blockbuster films or TV shows attain.

In the Seventies and Eighties I did a good deal of miscellaneous film work; those adventures, as I've said, must await the next volume of these reminiscences.

I had also, by this time, done a good deal of film journalism. I wrote a column for *American Film* that ran a couple of years. All this mass of opinion on movies and on Hollywood was collected in a book called *Film Flam*, a book that certainly would not have been published had *Lonesome Dove* not been such a huge hit.

There had been, in the Seventies, a considerable oil boom down in Texas. It stirred the community of Archer City; several members of my immediate family became, briefly, much richer than they had been.

With riches—even very temporary riches, came recklessness. Infidelity flourished, even in Archer City; various marriages floundered on the unlikely rocks of prosperity.

Everyone knows that booms, by definition, end, just as bubbles always burst. Seasoned oilmen know this, and seasoned bankers should; but, collectively, everyone forgets it until they awaken to the sound of mortgages failing and loans not being repaid.

As it happened, the Texas oil boom of the Seventies just edged into the Eighties before the scales began to fall off a great many overextended eyes. Then people who had just risen near enough to the middle class to invest in tennis lessons began to fall to earth and become working-class again.

Archer County had been organized in 1880. It was thought, as it was in many counties in that part of the country, that this grand event should have its memorial.

A pageant was created by a professional writer-producer of such pageants, and I came home from Washington, D.C., hoping to be entertained. And there was much to be entertained by, though the pageant-maker director himself should not be held responsible for most of it. Indians got tired of being scalped by cowboys and began to yank the cowboys off their horses and reverse the outcome.

When I was not watching the pageant I was being entertained by the louche behavior of the community generally. One thing everybody was doing was sweating—the heat wave crested at Fahrenheit 117, causing the fortunate cancellation of the planned marathon.

Taking this weird, wacko centennial celebration as my starting point I wrote a sequel to *The Last Picture Show* called *Texasville*. The book did fairly well, mainly because it came close on the heels of *Lonesome Dove*. A little later a film occurred, which will be discussed in due course.

28

As the Eighties ended Marcia and I began to see another end coming: the end of our bookshop in Georgetown. The kindly owners of the building we operated from could not last forever, and the building we were in was much too expensive for us.

With the help of my sister, Sue Deen, we had opened a tiny satellite of Booked Up, in the showroom of what had once been a Ford agency. It was called the Blue Pig Bookshop, after the famous blue pigs in *Lonesome Dove*.

When it became clear that Archer City, not Georgetown, was the future of the business, if it was to survive, I began to buy empty buildings, which were plentiful and cheap. By the time we had acquired three (of an eventual five) we gave up on Georgetown and brought all our stock to Archer City, where we became Booked Up for good. I began to buy the stock of booksellers who were going out of business, and I am still doing it. We have portions of about thirty bookshops now—as I reported in *Books*—and are still doing it, however quixotic the endeavor might be.

29

MOST WRITERS MY age have to come to grips with one persistent problem: they have to find something to write about that interests them
enough to make the investigation worth it. This priority is usually
experienced by writers with a long trail of books behind them, as I
have.

The book I was working on at this time was a strange half-autobio-
graphical piece called *Walter Benjamin at the Dairy Queen*. It was at the
local Dairy Queen, a few blocks below the mansion I had just acquired,
that I first began to read Walter Benjamin, particularly his thoughts about
storytelling, actually a study of Nikolai Leskov, but more general than that
sounds. The small-town Texas Dairy Queens at that time functioned, as
I explained, much like community centers, and were exactly the kind of
places that storytellers—unconscious that that is what they were—would
gossip and joke and pass on what local lore might have survived from
earlier times. (Very little has.)

Walter Benjamin argues that storytelling is a vanishing practice; vast
changes in world culture have to a degree made it obsolete.

At the time I had done an imperfect job of digesting Walter Benjamin—I laid the project aside, and aside it waited for some twenty years.

It hovered there, for two decades, never moving entirely out of sight. By the time it was finally finished I had had a heart attack and quadruple bypass surgery in Baltimore. I became a different person, but one of the few things I kept with me from what had come to seem like a former life was *Walter Benjamin at the Dairy Queen*, the storytelling and the stories that I personally might have to tell.

30

In the late Eighties I was mainly concerned with turning Archer City into a book town, rather on the model of Hay-on-Wye, the famous book town in Wales. I was also doing a lot of screenwriting, most of it for very quick money.

In Washington things were changing up the street at *The New Republic*, that long established journal of the Left. Our friend and first customer, Gilbert Harrison, who died in Scottsdale in 2008, sold the magazine to Martin Peretz, who rapidly hired, as literary editor, the subterraneanly famous Leon Wieseltier, who became a fast friend. Indeed, he became friend enough that for several years he used the third floor of Booked Up as his study. He seemed, and seems, to be about as well schooled as anyone can be, having studied, at one time or another, with Lionel Trilling and Meyer Shapiro at Columbia, Isaiah Berlin at Oxford, and such like folk. He was embarked, at the time, on a book sighing—I insist, sighing, not signing, though he's pretty adept at that too.

In the shuffle of papers on Leon's writing desk on our third floor there were scholarly papers on anesthesia and anesthesiology—as I was soon to discover for myself, in long operations the quality of the patient's sighing is important.

Aside from these journals the only things on Leon's writing table were a bottle of whiskey and a framed photograph of the French man of letters

Georges Bataille. Susan Sontag once stayed in that apartment, when we were doing something at the Folger. She looked at the picture and pronounced it to be a photograph of Georges Bataille; she reckoned that Leon kept it on his desk because he considered that that was where he ought to be coming from.

I have pondered that remark for years, without coming to any conclusion about Leon Wieseltier, Susan Sontag, or, for that matter, Georges Bataille, whose writing puts me to sleep, although I do know that, in a book called *Les Larmes de Eros*, there can be found a famous photograph of a Chinese criminal suffering the Death of One Thousand Cuts. This photograph has recently been reproduced in a book on Chinese punishments by Professors Timothy Brook, Jerome Bourgon, and Gregory Blue and published by Harvard University Press. In fact, according to the authors, the Death of One Thousand Cuts only involved four or five cuts and a neat stab to the heart. Whether Georges Bataille knew this fact I don't know.

Bataille or no Bataille, Leon was a pleasant guest to have slouching around in our upstairs. I was interested in observing the phenomenon of networking, as practiced at the highest level in D.C., Paris, London, and a few other capitals. Leon's only rival as a networker was the husband-wife team of Tim and Wren Wirth—Tim having twice been a senator from Colorado. Persons not known to Leon or the Wirths are probably people one should just not bother with—as the late Duke of Beauforth known as Master, might have said of the Lees-Milnes, James and Alvilde, who lived in his gate house at Badminton for a time, in the manner of Leon in Booked Up's third floor.

I enjoy networking but only as a spectator sport. One problem is that I immediately lose the phone numbers of almost everyone I know of any importance; and most of those whose numbers I don't lose are book scouts whom I can trust to find me anyway, when they have something to sell. Still, great networkers are fun to watch, even if one wouldn't want to bother with most of the people they know.

31

MOST PEOPLE WHO read this book will be aware, at least dimly, that there is an international freedom-to-write organization called PEN. Long ago, when such people as John Galsworthy, E. M. Forster, H. G. Wells, and other pure-minded souls were active in it, it was just called the PEN Club.

I myself, for most of my literary life, was largely unaware of PEN. I became a member and paid my dues but took no interest in PEN's programs—indeed, didn't have much of an idea what its programs were. I knew that around 1986 or so the PEN American Center, which I eventually led, had an international congress in New York, at which Norman Mailer, who was president of the New York center then, infuriated most of the women at the conference by mentioning that they were not intellectuals, like, say, Susan Sontag. Günter Grass and Saul Bellow had some kind of disagreement involving the South Bronx, a borough that, wisely perhaps, I have never visited.

I would have kind of liked to go to that congress and see all those literary stars, and I was living in Washington then, which was pretty close by. But I might as well have been living on Uranus, as far as PEN was concerned. I had, by then, won a Pulitzer Prize, but it made no difference and I soon passed on to do some chores in Hollywood. At the time of the much publicized congress I didn't have a single friend in the New York literary world. Even if I had been invited to the big shindig, I wouldn't have known who to talk to, or what to do.

32

Soon after that Susan Sontag, whom I had yet to meet came to my bookshop and bought two books by Laura Riding, but I was not in the shop that day and missed her. As president of the PEN American Center, succeding Mailer, Susan created at least as many controversies as Mailer had but I didn't find this out until I had to deal with the bitter harvest of some of them.

I was, meanwhile, building my book town in West Texas—the contentions of the New York literary world seemed very distant. I had never done a single chore for PEN but when glasnost showed up and a few Russian writers were brought to America in the wake of Gorbachev's visit, I was asked to help with a reading at the Folger Library.

These Russian writers had only recently, remember, been let out into the light of Western sunshine. Though Joseph Brodsky, just back from getting his Nobel Prize, stayed with us all day and helped out as best he could, the Russians were, nevertheless, condescended to over and over again, not least on a morning visit to the Folger, where they were taken into the vaults and shown the *Laws* of Catherine the Great—the book was held at a distance of about ten feet. It would have been better, in my view, to take the book up, rather than bringing the Russians down into what probably looked to them like a very up-to-date prison. I was embarrassed for them, exposed in their shabbiness to Western *snobisme* at its most extreme.

Lunch at *The New Republic* went a little better. I then snuck a few of the men off to my bookshop, where they could touch the books, and also have a few beers.

That evening at the Folger I read with Daniil Granin, who, as a boy of eighteen, had commanded a tank battalion during the siege of Leningrad, holding his line for one thousand days. He was probably the oldest of the visiting Russians. I liked him a lot.

Karen Kennerly, the executive director of the PEN American Center, seemed to like my performance at the Folger, while perhaps not noticing how much I didn't like the whole proceedings. The next time I heard from her it was to ask me to read yet again. This reading was held at the U.N., I forget the cause. Norman Mailer wore battle scars—his wife had slugged him, he announced proudly. We went over to the U.N. on the subway, the first and only time I have ridden the New York subway. Susan Sontag came along—we met but glancingly.

I was given a passage from one of Václav Havel's *Letters to Olga*, which mentioned the name of a French philosopher named Levinas, of whom I had never heard. It didn't matter.

The crowd at the U.N. was not vast but it was respectable and none of us disgraced ourselves.

Later I looked up the works of M. Levinas and found them quite opaque.

Later still, at a dinner at Katharine Graham's, I met Václav Havel himself. His country was now free. He did his best with the Georgetown crowd but looked as though he would rather be outside, having a smoke.

In order to spread him around I ate dinner at his table, but, for dessert, was asked to move one table away so that others could enjoy the rather raspy responses of the new president of the Czech Republic.

Actually I was glad to move. Havel was under heavy constraint, as any-one would be at one of Mrs. Graham's dinners, many of which, like this one, were semi–state dinners, Reagan having evidently decided not to put on a show for the Czechs.

I also liked the table switch because Pamela Harriman, greatest *hori-zontale* of her era, was just across from me. Though we were neighbors in Georgetown for many years, and I knew of her extraordinary history, it was the one and only time I sat at table with her.

33

AROUND THIS TIME Leon Wieseltier began to sound rather like a stalking horse whenever I was around and PEN was mentioned. But whom was he stalking for, and why? He seemed to be wondering who of his acquaintance might make a good president of PEN, the last thing I would be wondering about if I were as networked as he.

I was not too helpful, mostly because the notion that *I* might become president of PEN seemed like an absurdist joke. PEN's New York office is at Prince and Broadway—I had been in it only once, for a few minutes, before the reading at the U.N., prior to which, except for the reading with the Russians, the only contact I had ever had with a literary organization was to go to a few dinners with the Texas Institute of Letters, which didn't enlighten me much. Judging from such scanty evidence as I then had, literary societies spent a certain amount of time making virtuous pronouncements, and spent the rest of the time congratulating themselves for obscure feats of one sort or another.

Famously, about this time, the Iranian cleric the Ayatollah Khomeini shocked or at least startled the literary world by issuing his famous fatwa calling for the death of Salman Rushdie, who wrote a book called *The Satanic Verses*, a book that greatly upset much of the vast and touchy Muslim world.

I was twiddling my fingers in Albuquerque when this news broke, trying to buy a bookstore. Had I bought it, I would have stayed in New Mexico to pack it, missing a day of fervor and fun in New York, where PEN
was summoning lots of writers—most of whom were a lot closer to the
Rushdie action than Albuquerque. There were to be protests by various
and sundry to answer this enormity.

My bookstore deal fell through, and though a little mystified by being
overnight included in a group from which so recently I had been excluded,
I went. Many fervent pronouncements were made; so far at least Salman
Rushdie got saved. Probably the British Secret Service was largely responsible for this. Though at the meeting Gay Talese recited the Lord's Prayer,
which may have helped.

34

I SUPPOSE I went to that protest meeting to see what a protest meeting in New York—one with a literary basis—was like. My voice meant nothing. I was a midlist novelist who had gotten lucky with the movies, that's all. I knew that during the high years of the civil rights movement, or the low years of the Vietnam War, there were frequent and worthy protests, and most of the writers I liked, such as Norman Mailer, seemed to be on the same side as I was. I even did a lunch counter sit-in in Houston, while teaching at Rice. It was the right thing to do, although I don't think it made anyone in Houston either more or less racist

Though I did, as I'll relate, serve for two years as president of the PEN American Center, I've never quite shaken off my feeling that writers in their public-protest mode seem a little silly. If they are good writers, and many were, their pages, their sentences and paragraphs, have a potency that the protests never reach. Nor are they necessarily good describers of the follies they are attempting to alleviate or prevent. Time after time, at such gatherings, I found myself wishing I was just at home, reading the very people who were declaiming away right in front of me.

I suppose it's a quirk but if so it's a quirk that makes me peculiarly un-suited to run an organization of a sort that I was soon to be president of.

35

EXCEPT FOR GAY Talese's fine recitation of the Lord's Prayer, I remember almost nothing of the protest I had flown from Albuquerque to join. Norman Mailer mentioned nonpejoratively (he later explained) that Tom Wolfe was at the time the publishing world's flavor of the month.

Carl Bernstein, who didn't speak, called his publisher, Robert Bernstein, to ask him to yank his just released new book about his family off the shelves, a suggestion that probably died in the reception room of Random House.

For me the happiest aspect of the Rushdie protest was that I ran into my old friend Greg Curtis on the airplane going back. He was then editor in chief of *Texas Monthly*. We did four hours of catching up as the plane ground its way back to Dallas. Salman Rushdie wasn't mentioned. Later I read *Midnight's Children* and thought it a near-great book. *The Satanic Verses* I never got through, but that doesn't mean the author deserved to have his life put at threat.

36

BY MY OWN reckoning I had not exactly shone at this gathering of the righteous and so did not expect to hear from PEN again, a snap judgment that turned out to be incorrect.

A few months later I was in my ranch house in Texas, trying to figure out how to cram a few more books into it: it contained about twelve thousand at the time—when the phone rang. George Braziller, a distinguished publisher whose lists I have always admired, and who was, moreover, a friend of my first agent, Dorothea Oppenheimer, a fellow European with similar tastes, was on the line.

George Braziller asked me point-blank if I would agree to be president of the PEN American Center for a span of two years, a question so unexpected that I might have followed the example of the second Mrs. Woodrow Wilson, when President Wilson finally got around to proposing to her, causing her to promptly fall out of bed.

Fortunately I wasn't in bed and ran no risk of falling out, but it was a shock anyway. Me? President of PEN, an office held by Norman Mailer and Susan Sontag? (Along with some obscure others.)

First off, I needed to know why PEN would want me. On this issue George Braziller was not particularly enlightening; he was too polite (or too smart) to mention that crowds of famous writers were not rushing down to Prince Street to offer up their freedoms in order to take what might be considered a thankless job, which involved, to begin with, riding herd on a swollen board of mostly Jews but with a sprinkling of East Coast WASPs and one (always absent) Palestinian, the late Edward Said.

Fortunately I had read, in my years as a reviewer, most of the books produced by the PEN board—indeed, I had most of their works in my library—but I had probably met less than half a dozen sitting board members: a variegated crowd of scribblers, to say the least.

That very fact—that I was a tabula rasa—might have been why I was offered the president's job. Maybe I would be able to operate above the seething quarrels, some of which had long historical roots.

In my startlement I put George Braziller off—give me a day, I said, and he did. I had mainly been planning to shore up my bookshop—the local branch at length—and Woody and Fran, my two Vermonters, had just settled into my big house for a job that would likely take them two years. What would I be doing, during this time, other than getting in their way? That there would be culture clashes was certain. Vermonters are not much like Texans, and Woody—the only carpenter I know to make his own translation of the *Iliad*—could be expected to tolerate only so much *Texasisme*. I myself can tolerate only so much of it, and did not really want to stay around trying to cram books into the ranch house for two years.

So I took the job, becoming the first non–New York president of PEN since Booth Tarkington, who held the post at the very beginning of the existence of an American PEN.

Why did I accept a job I didn't feel in the least suited for? Was it because I sincerely believed in the principles of PEN? Well, I believed that writers should be free to write what they want without being punished for it. There were no doubt tributary principles but I was soon so busy that I didn't give them much thought.

Mainly, I think, I took the job because it gave me a reason for really spending time in New York City. I had been in and out of Manhattan for decades, but mostly in one- and two-day jaunts in which I scouted books. I knew the bookshops, but didn't know the city. I could easily have missed PEN but missing New York was another thing. The chance to get to know one of the greatest of the world's cities was what decided me. I took the job.

37

KAREN KENNERLY, WHO became and remains a close friend, had been the executive director of the American PEN Center for a very long time. She came down to D.C. to brief me on the labyrinth of projects and committees that PEN had going at the time, some of them new, many of ancient growth.

Although her briefing was expert, my eyes tend to glaze over when I'm told stuff. My normal practice involves *inventing* characters, which was unnecessary at PEN, since most of the board members had already invented themselves. When I first entered it, the noisy space at Broadway and Prince seemed like a world-class aviary; there was, for sure, a lot of plumage.

For a time I was dispatched by Karen to separate but equal lunches with the heads of various more or less warring comittees. Everyone but myself seemed to have long settled and passionately held views on what PEN should or should not be doing. I had no opinion on most of these issues—where, indeed, would I have gotten one?—and decided that a cautious neutrality offered my best hope.

The most interesting of my lunches was with Donald Barthelme, the sharp Texas postmodernist whom I had somehow never met, although we had crisscrossed with one another in Houston for many years, never meeting unless it was glancingly; neither of us could remember for sure. I think Don had once been passionate about PEN and its politics, but by the time we met for lunch he was sick and had mainly lost interest. He had just time left in which to establish a first-rate writing program at the University of Houston. I saw him once more, at a Texas Institute of Letters banquet where he was given a Life Achievement award—it was richly deserved, in my view. He said that night that writing had enabled him to have a splendid life—and so it has for me as well.

38

MOST OF THE infighting I witnessed at PEN has fallen out of my memory—a rather senior memory now, and, as it gets more senior, the less reliable it is—which, after all, is the common way.

The major debate I more or less moderated during my two years at PEN was a big PEN, little PEN debate. Some wanted PEN to grow in wealth and influence, and others wanted it to stay small, and, I guess, cozy—in my view the prospects for cozy were extremely limited. For most of its history in America PEN was, of necessity, a small PEN. For some years it lived in a room or two at the Knickerbocker Club. The offices it eventually moved into on lower Broadway were the equivalent of a cold water flat. The bathroom was a long trot down the hall.

It soon became apparent that the small PEN that had long existed was the PEN many members would prefer. Perhaps unfairly, because I knew so little, I came to identify the Little Englanders on the board with some folks who lived on 11th Street, or had, or might. These would include Kirkpatrick and Faith Sale (the latter an editor for a while of the elusive Thomas Pynchon, the former an ecological reformist and historian); the short story writer Grace Paley, Donald Barthelme in his New York years, and maybe more that I cannot accurately place, geographically. (About the first thing I did after leaving PEN was to blurb Kirk Sale's excellent book

The Conquest of Paradise. A book about the devastation that followed the arrival of Columbus in the West Indies.)

The late Faith Sale, during my time at PEN, headed the Freedom to Write Committee, perhaps the most important of the PEN committees.

Those on the board who wanted to see a PEN that had more influence, presumably for the good, recognized that this would require an elevation in style; it also, obviously, meant raising a lot more money. It meant patrons, it meant fund-raising galas—the two I presided over were both staged by Tina Brown, then in her *New Yorker* years—and it might mean, as Karen Kennerly and others hoped, a foundation of some sort to help PEN with . . . with . . . with what?

What PEN really wanted its foundation to provide was what every other struggling nonprofit wants: money with no strings attached. And, moreover, *clean* money—money with no blood on it.

That, as any professional fund-raiser will tell you, is a lot to ask. It was very hard to find money with no blood on it, and, if you should get lucky and *find* it, the people who have it probably won't give it to you. I was dismal at raising money—this could have been predicted. I raised directly, in two years, only $1,000—a gift from Oveta Culp Hobby, in Houston.

I wasn't good at galas, either, being inexpert in the delicate metropolitan matter of *placement.* At my second gala, held downtown in the old Customs House, both Susan Sontag and Peter Jennings (the late ABC anchor) left because they were seated with people who had no idea who they were. Such, I suppose, is the Big Time. Towering figures such as Susan Sontag and Peter Jennings *must* be seated next to people who want to sit beneath a tower. What could be more simple?

Silly as it all sounds—and much of it *was* silly—the struggle within PEN over what kind of PEN it was to be just happened to become particularly intense during my two terms. (I could have honorably left at the end of my first year, but my house wasn't finished, and I had not had enough of New York. So I stayed, accomplishing naught.)

I didn't care whether PEN was small or large, weak or powerful, but, in as much as I was the first president from the heartland since Booth Tarkington, I did think that I might just make some effort to involve PEN members or branches who didn't live between the Hudson and the East Rivers, or the boroughs just beyond, in what might be called Greater USA.

To this end I soon headed out for the territory, visiting Berkeley, Chicago, and Boston, trying to beat a drum that was essentially illusionary. PEN had neither the money nor the interest to do much about the provinces.

I decided, next, to try a series of readings, each one involving writers from a particular region. We started with the Pacific Northwest and that one actually went fairly well. Kathy Dunn, Ken Kesey, Barry Lopez, and others performed quite respectably, producing, in me at least, a false optimism that did not survive reading number two: writers from the Great Plains.

PEN had invited Richard Ford, Frederick Manfred, Larry Woiwode, and others, and Ford and Woiwode read well, but Fred Manfred, who is not a poet, read his poetry and essentially sank the whole series. He was six foot eight and in his eighties, which didn't keep him from giving the office girls a lively chase.

I had thought maybe to go on to the Southwest, or maybe the Great Lakes area, but the Great Plains produced such a miserable evening that

I gave up, aside from a pointless trip to Houston to see if it might serve as a site for some future congress or conference. Since all I managed to rake up for PEN was Mrs. Hobby's $1,000, that effort, too, died on the vine.

In this particular incident not enough of my heart was ever in it. I like to read what writers write but am rarely in the mood to listen to them yap.

39

I SHOULD HAVE mentioned earlier that PEN's primary patrons, during the first year that I was president, were Saul and Gayfryd Steinberg, who at this time were very rich: rich enough that Gayfryd could cheerfully spend a million dollars on a birthday party for Saul.

By the time I more or less got settled in at PEN I had met Gayfryd Steinberg only once, at one of our galas. On Gayfryd, mainly, it seemed, rested our hopes for a helpful foundation coming into being, a prospect that made many members of the PEN board vocally restive.

Was the Steinbergs' money too bloody for PEN? One who definitely thought it was was new board member Ken Auletta, a distinguished reporter for *The New Yorker* and other journals who reported on finance, the entertainment business, and the like. This was a time when money-men on the order of Ivan Boesky and Michael Miliken were going to jail.

Ken Auletta issued a sharp little protest about the Steinbergs' involvement with PEN, which I read while on an airplane flying to Hollywood, where I hoped to get a job. Had I been flying east, rather than west, I probably would have called Ken Auletta up, invited him to lunch, and he and I would have made a private peace, which would have no effect at all on the climate at PEN, where, it was clear, there would soon be blood on the floor, as well as on the money.

Rather than inviting Ken to lunch I wrote him a letter, which, not to my surprise, ended up in *New York* magazine. I had come to realize what I really always knew, which is that people as cynical as myself should not involve themselves too deeply in the nonprofit world.

The result for PEN was, first of all, the loss of Gayfryd. I came back from Hollywood in time to preside over a rather stormy board meeting. Gayfryd Steinberg left us, changed her mind and came back, then (I think) turned on her heels and left again. I recall one meeting in the executive dining room of Simon and Schuster at which Gayfryd arrived wearing a shirt so diaphanous that she was essentially topless. Others at the meeting were Dick Snyder (my publisher and other head of Simon and Schuster), Karen, and Gayfryd and her nipples.

Up to this point I had not seen enough of Gayfryd Steinberg to know whether or not I liked her. Bureaucratically it soon ceased to matter. The Steinbergs suffered a reversal of fortune, Saul had a stroke, and there were no more million-dollar birthday parties.

At PEN the clamor for a foundation soon sank to whispers. There is, as of this writing, no PEN Foundation. The document hammered out before my time, which was supposed to entice patrons, was, as Dick Snyder pointed out, so plainly reluctant that few tough-minded, thick-skinned New York patrons-to-be would have been likely to write PEN too many checks.

40

MORE FUN, FOR me, than the rancorous board meetings at Broadway and Prince were the meetings of International PEN, which, during my time with the organization, met in Maastricht, Toronto-Montreal, Madeira, etc. At these august, not to say pompous, gatherings an occasional world-class writer was likely to show up: Chinua Achebe in Maastricht, Wole Soyinka in Toronto, Harold Pinter and Lady Antonia Fraser everywhere.

Susan Sontag, who was the president I succeeded, had made a bevy of enemies which I—mild, uncombative, bored—soothed to some extent. The one person who never got soothed was my friend the novelist-activist Meredith Tax, who, despite unending efforts, could never quite get PEN, or the world, to treat women a whole lot better than had been the world's custom, and, on the whole, still is.

The person I found most fun to watch in International PEN was the international secretary Alexander Blok. (I would assume Alex is some relation to the famous Russian poet of the same name, but maybe not.) I admired Alex mainly because he drove the agenda so ruthlessly in a waterfall of French that we all got to go eat a good deal sooner, and dining well soon came, for me, to be the main point. (I knew before I took the post that I wasn't really a good citizen, a fact I only faked tolerably well.)

Philip Roth said the same thing of himself when my term was ending and he was offered the job.

41

I COULD NOT have considered accepting the presidency of American PEN had I not been reasonably flush at the time. I came to PEN in the year that the miniseries of *Lonesome Dove* made its very successful release on CBS. My friend and publisher Bill Wittliff wrote the script and co-produced the film.

Though I didn't benefit directly from *Lonesome Dove* I did benefit collaterally, in the way of jobs in Hollywood and better deals for my books. I bought a few bookshops that were clearly approaching the end of their days, and I felt free, as president of PEN, to reside at the Hotel Pierre, my hotel in New York since my first trip there—Dorothea Oppenheimer probably recommended it.

This may have been insensitive, considering how poor PEN was, but I was paying my own way and, the work being pretty exhausting to one not used to it, I wanted a reliable place to lay my head when it was finally time to.

I have never been good with groups, and the PEN board, to its credit, was a fervent and passionate group. I admired their passion but never shared it: I'm just too much of a Hobbesian.

I also came to realize—what the board didn't realize—that they were less an organization than a tribe: the tribe of New York writers whose queen, though just then out of the teepee, was Susan Sontag.

After all, I had just traveled across the country, from Berkeley to Boston, to get writers in those highly literate locales to come to Broadway and Prince and participate. Few did, partly because we couldn't afford to bring them, and partly because they had only a faint interest in what went on at the home office.

What I thought, when I finished my first board meeting and what I thought later, when I finished my last, is that PEN American houses essentially a New York PEN. Every time I think about it I recall a long lost book by Ford Maddox Ford, called *New York Is Not America*. Well, one could argue that it is and it isn't. But it's certainly not *just*, or even *mostly*, the America that I know.

At PEN I found myself in the odd position of being chief of a tribe I had never belonged to. Did I want to belong to it, really?

It was PEN itself that inadvertently convinced me that, whether I wanted to or not, I could never be a member of the PEN tribe of New York city.

Why? Because I didn't live there, and thus could not claim to be one of the People. Less than two years before I was made president I was sort of unimaginable at PEN; and much less than two years after I left I was unimaginable again. I did not live in New York and thus could not be one of the People. Within a month of my departure the secretaries at PEN ceased to know even my name.

In the end—in and out though I was—I believe I learned more about PEN than PEN ever learned about me.

Considering all the circumstances, it could not have been otherwise.

42

WHEN SUSAN SONTAG first came to Texas to visit me, I was still crammed with my twelve thousand books into my family ranch house in southeast Archer County. On her first visit she came alone; on her second and final visit she came with her son, David Rieff.

We had become fast (and expensive) friends during my tenure at PEN, which involved, every Sunday night, dining at Petrossian, the elegant American offshoot of the famous Parisian caviar restaurant.

Susan drank pepper vodka and ate a lot of fish eggs. Between us we may have hastened the demise of the sturgeon in various seas, though of course the Russian mob helped.

During my first year at PEN we scarcely met, except at Petrossian, and talked mainly about what we'd read. Then I'd put her in a cab and set her off to I knew not where, after which I'd stroll the few blocks to my hotel.

Susan was close, at the time, to the photographer Annie Leibovitz, who, when I was briefly famous because of *Picture Show*, showed up like the woodsprite she then resembled and photographed me in an alley beside the bookshop, probably for *Rolling Stone*. The next time I saw Annie was many years later, when she turned up with Susan for a reading my partner, Diana Ossana, and I gave at the 92nd Street Y.

Backstage there was a lot of sushi, but no one noticed it except Calvin Trillin, who was there to introduce us. He promptly ate all the food, as is his habit.

On Susan's first visit to Archer City, when it was tending toward dinnertime, we collected Woody and Fran, my two carpenters, and drove to Wichita Falls, where we dined at a fairly lively honky-tonk called the Bar L. Unlike every other Texas honky-tonk I've visited, the Bar L sported a Polynesia frieze—though an eatery less Polynesian than the Bar L would be difficult to imagine.

Fortunately the Bar L served one of Susan Sontag's favorite dishes: chicken gizzards. Not knowing when she would meet a chicken gizzard again, she had two orders, I believe, attacking those gizzards with an abandon previously reserved for beluga caviar.

On the way home we happened to pass a little dirt track where stock-car races were held. As we passed, the roar of the cars was raspy and loud. The roar alerted Susan, who asked if we could stop and watch.

Certainly we could and we did. As we piled out of my car and headed for the ticket office I heard Susan, excited, say "Oh, wow!"

Oh wow?

The world intellectual shed her highbrow trappings for a moment and became a big, excited American girl who was on her way to watch the cars!

When I think of Susan Sontag now, dead three years, it's that moment and that "Oh, wow!" that comes to mind first—it's a kind of highwater mark in my relations with Susan, though I continued to see her with some regularity once my time at PEN ended. After the success of her historical novel, *The Volcano Lover*, she acquired a penthouse on West 24th Street.

I was only in it once and spent my whole visit looking at her library—as she herself had done the first time she was in my library. Booked Up, my shop, had just bought a couple thousand of Susan's books, European paperbacks, mostly; these had long been in storage and I was anxious to see what she had left, which was a lot. (The books on 24th Street, along with her archive, went to UCLA.)

The next time Susan came to visit me in Texas there was a bit of a mix-up at the airport in Dallas. I was there with time to spare but Susan's secretary had changed the flight number and I waited several gates away. The mishap took maybe fifteen minutes to sort out, but however long it was it was long enough for Susan's profound conviction of abandonment to seize her. David, her son, was there and I was very soon there, explaining what had gone wrong. It did little good. I had inadvertently touched the deepest pain in her psyche; that easily triggered conviction of abandonment.

I rushed them the few miles to Ponder, to the steak house where I had been eating just before I saw the old bus and found the title for *Lonesome Dove*.

David Rieff is an authority on the Texas boot, and had co-authored a book on the subject. He went off next door to get a pair of boots made by a bootmaker he approved. Susan calmed down and ate a steak; but I think the calming was only on the surface. I continued to see her, when we were both in New York, for several years, but I think it was no go, really. I could never lure her to the book town again, even when I purchased a splendid bunch of Polish books. I had thought I was pretty vigilant about protecting Susan from her own darknesses, and intellectually she forgave my slip. But looking deeper, I don't think so. In a way there was no room for error with Susan. I recall an odd blip that occurred one evening when we were having our usual meal at Petrossian. I don't remember anything untoward happening, but, when she had settled into her taxi, she looked at me and said, "Don't ever do that again." I was startled and in a flash the taxi left. I didn't know what I had done that I was never to do again.

In this case the disfavor wasn't lasting, since the following week, we had the same meal at the same place and nothing was said about the incident at all. But I had seen, in Texas, the child at the airport whose parents had not been where they were supposed to be.

The last time I spoke to her she was recuperating from her fight with the uterine sarcoma that preceded by a few years the cancer that killed her. She was in the VIP wing of Presbyterian Hospital in New York and I sent her some caviar.

I don't get to New York much anymore but when I do I find it's Susan I miss the most. Her spirit and large figure hover over certain parts of town, as Balzac and his spirit hover over Paris. Balzac was a great writer and Susan wasn't, but, in my short time in Manhattan she was the omnipresent figure: in the theaters and opera houses; at the ballet, off to the movies and the museums, galleries, public forums of all kinds, photography shows. She stood out, somehow, against the skyline and it's unfortunate that she got herself involved, from a distance, with the tragic alteration of that skyline by the events of 9/11.

In my opinion the last essays that Susan Sontag wrote—on translation, on Victor Serge, on Leonid Tsypkin and his *Summer in Baden-Baden*, in *Regarding the Pain of Others*, were her richest writings. *Illness as Metaphor* is an important polemic, but the last pieces carry her to a new depth.

Her first triumph, *Against Interpretation*, seems dated now—Susan was jousting with a windmill that had already fallen over of its own weight. Much as she may have read initially—and that was a lot—her curiosity and her insight deepened and linked up near the end. If I had to choose two of her books to take with me to the proverbial desert island they would be *Where the Stress Falls* and *At the Same Time*, with *On Photography* maybe as a chaser.

A lifetime of reading and looking went into those essays.

Susan said to me once that she had been too good a student. I had been teasing her at the time, trying to dissuade her from her lifelong habit of grading.

"Susan, you can't possibly know that this is the second best Uruguayan novel," a challenge that she always rose to, hotly defending her choices. Her attitude reminds me of something Leon Wieseltier says of another top student, Harold Bloom. "Harold feels that all literature should pass before him and get a grade," Leon said.

The serious side to all Susan's grading was that excellent grades produced mobility. And Susan had it. Nearly every day I walk or drive past Susan Sontag's childhood home, on Drachman Street, just east of Tucson Boulevard. The house doesn't look as if it's changed much since the day in the Forties when she and her family left it for L.A.

It was from L.A. that she launched her ascent of the great universities of America and Europe. Great grades meant movement, and she moved, and moved quickly and always upward and upward, until she hit the roof of the academic tower. When, ruefully, she said to me that she had been *too* good a student I think she meant that she now recognized that a report card filled with straight As from the best schools in the world didn't necessarily take you far, or make you much, in the more exacting world outside the ivied walls.

43

My term at PEN ended in June 1991. I was never happier than when the great airplane took off, to deposit me, soon, in West Texas, where I was expecting to have a relaxed summer. Woody and Fran were still finding last-minute things to do to the big house, but that wouldn't last much longer. Then I would take my time emptying books from the ranch house into the big house, a carful at a time.

It didn't turn out that way. My son, James, had issued his acclaimed first album, *Too Long in the Wasteland*, the year before but had later run into political problems with his second album. Having risen higher with one record than anyone might have expected, he was under some pressure to follow up that success with another album just as good.

My summer of relaxation turned out to be nearer the worst of times than it was to the best. My mother was crazy, my sisters variously stressed. In the bust that followed the oil boom my brother's welding business diminished to such an extent that he decided to go back to school and get a doctorate in English studies, which, in time, he did.

While at PEN I had managed to scratch out a short and simple little novel about Calamity Jane, called *Buffalo Girls*, which later was made into a truly bizarre movie.

While trying to think of something to write I decided to indulge my passion for sequels and launched into a fourth volume of the *Terms of Endearment* tetralogy, this one to be called *The Evening Star*. The writing went well right up until the day I had a heart attack. It was a small cardiac event, as such things go, and might have occurred several days, or even a week or more, before it was discovered.

The story of my heart attack and its consequences are related fully in *Walter Benjamin at the Dairy Queen*; it need not be reprised here. Eventually either myself or my ghost or some combination of the two produced more than twenty more books, most of them novels but some of them nonfiction.

There was, for example, a short biography of Crazy Horse, and a similarly short study of Buffalo Bill and Annie Oakley.

Then I edited a book of short fiction about the American West, 1950 to the present, and called *Still Wild*. I became interested in hundred-victim massacres in the Old West and produced a study of them called *Oh What a Slaughter*.

Then wanderlust seized me—we are in the Nineties now. First I ran the American Interstate highways for a while, producing a book called *Roads*. But the continent couldn't hold me. I flew over to Tahiti, one of the loveliest places on earth, and took a freighter to the distant Marquesas, returning to Archer City a few hours before my mother died, which was more or less as I had expected.

Finally, where nonfiction went, I gathered up the various pieces I had done, under Barbara Epstein's guidance, and published them as *Sacagawea's Nickname*.

All this plus the post-surgical screenwriting I did with my screenwriting partner, Diana Ossana; before we knew it we had done twelve scripts, and were soon to have the luck of a lifetime when we obtained the rights to Annie Proulx's great short story "Brokeback Mountain," which won us each a screenwriting Oscar.

44

For reasons I can't fathom, and perhaps don't really need to fathom, both as reader and writer I have long been attracted to tetralogies. Lawrence Durrell's *Alexandria Quartet* was probably the first to really grab me, perhaps because of the huge success of the first book, *Justine*.

Then, by accident, I happened on to the Ford Maddox Ford Tietjens books, which I liked very much in spots, but only in spots; the author, it seemed to me, had carried his story one volume too far, which still puts him with a slight edge on Anthony Powell, whose *A Dance to the Music of Time* is at least two books too long, and now very dated to boot.

Powell's long novel is in twelve parts, as is his friend (if he had friends) James Lees-Milne's wonderful *Diaries*, which is nearly as novelistic as *A Dance*, as I hope to argue someday.

Lately, to my own surprise, my own *Last Picture Show* sequence (*The Last Picture Show, Texasville, Duane's Depressed, When the Light Goes,* and *Rhino Ranch*) unexpectedly turned itself into a quintet. The last two books, *When the Light Goes* and *Rhino Ranch*, are about the coming of age. They carry Duane—just eighteen when I first took an interest in his life—on to his end.

* * *

The novelist, when he sets out to judge his own output, has no special authority—this has been pointed out by many writers.

Probably most strangers, coming to my work, would follow popular opinion and declare *Lonesome Dove* their favorite.

It's certainly a book with some power, and part of the power comes from the fact that we're retracing a myth—the myth of the cowboy, or of the American West as a whole. My father and his brothers, all cattlemen, served that myth all their lives, and I, as a descendant of cattlemen, was always aware of it but long ago fled from it.

I don't dislike *Lonesome Dove* and I was not surprised that the book did so well from the prize point of view, not to mention the sales point of view. The book has reinforced the myth by being made into an extremely appealing and successful miniseries, which will achieve its twentieth anniversary this year. It got a grip on the public imagination like no other Western of its time.

What I learned from writing it was that myth is tenacious. Any attempt to deromanticize the cowboy will only boomerang and end up striking whatever it attempts to debunk. If *Lonesome Dove* satisfies its huge public emotionally, then the author should just stand back and let it happen. It does no harm, and may even provide a kind of security.

45

ONE CRITICAL PROJECT that originated with Simon and Schuster and, almost at once, faltered, seems to me worth mentioning. Simon and Schuster proposed to publish my works in a new, classy line of trade paperbacks, with lively covers and brief introductions by myself. By this time they had acquired rights to the few titles they hadn't published themselves and were all set to roll.

Someone, possibly Dr. Johnson, said that a man was a fool to write prose for anything but money, so I asked for a modest fee and got it.

I welcomed this opportunity to review my own works—very few authors *wouldn't* welcome it. It was, in a small way, like the opportunity Henry James was offered when Scribners decided to bring out the New York Edition, and to illustrate it with the somber photographs by Alvin Langdon Coburn. (Ironically the set is very expensive now, not because of Henry James's great ruminative Prefaces but because collectors so yearn for Coburn's splendid photographs. This is an irony Henry James was fortunate to miss. All that smart talk about the novels, which forms a kind of cornerstone of critical theory, was not really much wanted then, and certainly isn't much wanted now, whereas the great photographs rise at every sale.)

*   *   *

I at once started writing *my* modest prefaces. I worked backward from what I was doing at the time, which happened to be *The Desert Rose*. Then I did *Cadillac Jack* and *Somebody's Darling*; then, out of sequence, I jumped back to *All My Friends Are Going to Be Strangers* and *In a Narrow Grave*. There's also a little seen issue of *Moving On*, in plain wrappers, but then momentum seems to have been lost. I soon learned that my attention span, where my own fiction is concerned, is very short. Earlier on I felt intense about by fiction, but I had a period, around the time I went to PEN, when I approached it more casually: the mode in which I wrote *Boone's Lick*, *Anything for Billy*, *Buffalo Girls*—all essentially frontier yarns, with moments in each that tend toward parody; *Anything for Billy* essentially is parody—a parody of a dime novel.

I was enjoying writing my prefaces, which I knew were light *belles lettres*. But, all of a sudden, the wind shifted at Simon and Schuster: they still wanted the prefaces, but they didn't want to pay for them. They wanted me to do them for free. No clear reason was ever given for this policy decision. They just didn't want to pay for any more prefaces.

I found this irritating. My prefaces were only trifles, but they were sprightly trifles. I was only being paid $1,000 a preface, which doesn't seem like much. The sequence stopped at (I believe) seven.

46

I HAVE MENTIONED in various contexts that I consider the formation of my large library, now swelling past thirty thousand volumes and filling three houses, one a very large house at that, to be an achievement equal to if not better than my writings themselves.

Remember that I started with *no* books—no Peter Rabbit, no Grimm and Andersen, no Little Red Riding Hood, no nothing.

Then, at age six, I acquired nineteen books.

Then, once in college in Houston, I discovered the world of antiquarian bookshops, where I've lived, to the extent that it's still possible, ever since.

Between 1954 and 1962 I formed three more or less shabby libraries. The first was filled with too many books by Romain Rolland. I can't recall exactly what became of this library. I think I quietly abandoned it, in one of my many moves as a young man. It was a beginner's library and its loss was no big deal.

About that time—when my first library ceased to interest me—I moved to San Francisco and, bookwise, started over. From my beginner's library I retain one book, a copy of Ezra Pound's *ABC of Reading*, which I acquired just before I abandoned the library it was meant to be part of. I kept the *ABC* and read it several times—it was really, I see now, an ABC to modernism, which suited me fine.

The reader might well ask why this account of the expanding and shrinking of my various libraries matters at all.

I could give several answers to that question but the simplest is that you write what you've read, to a large degree—and, just as importantly, you write what you will someday *reread*. I am now entering the time of rereading and am assembling the one hundred books or so that I keep with me to reread as long as I'm here. These are the books that, over about six decades, have meant the most to me; it is because of their combined weight and tone that I have become the kind of writer I now am.

As a bookseller and writer I have had the good luck to see and explore three very large personal libraries: those of Huntington Cairns, Joseph Alsop, and Susan Sontag.

Huntington Cairns had no idea how many books he owned, so we counted and came out at about sixteen thousand. Joe Alsop thought he had sixteen thousand when in fact he had a little more than nine thousand. Susan Sontag, the one time I saw her library, flung her arms wide and said, "I have everything." It was a bravura gesture because she had been in Archer City and knew that I had more—but having more doesn't mean that I've read them as intelligently or pondered them as deeply.

Readers with large libraries often get asked whether they have read every book on the shelves—to which Susan and I have roughly the same answer: We've *considered* and consideration can vary from day to day and book to book. One can consider and not read or consider and read.

Large as these three libraries are, they are nothing compared to the immense gathering of the British polymath C. K. Ogden, who had about eighty thousand books, and *that* pales beside Michael Foot's 120,000 (I get these figures from the late librarian Lawrence Clark Powell, who, I believe, purchased both libraries for UCLA. Susan Sontag's library now lives beside them.)

Umberto Ecco is said to have thirty thousand volumes too.

47

FORTUNATELY THE TIME in which I began my long hunt for the books that now form my library was a sort of golden era for adventurous book accumulators—accumulation is a better word than collection when it comes to describing the miscellany that I have. There were then more than one thousand bookshops spread across the land—115 in Los Angeles, for example, and, in 1950, still 175 in New York city. Chicago, too, was a great book town then, and likewise Philadelphia, Boston, and various other places.

How I came to acquire literary taste at all remains a mystery to me. My parents were indifferent to books, and, indeed, to taste itself, although my father might admire a fine saddle. But taste of a broader sort would have fallen very low in their catalogue of values.

By browsing in, considering, and often rejecting a given book in a given bookshop I gradually came to have some confidence. I knew what pleased my eye. I like well-designed books, with a clear typeface and attractive, if simple, binding.

I've been in the hunt nearly sixty years, during which time much has changed in the world of books. But a casual visitor to my home, one who knew at least a little bit about books, would eventually come to suspect that all these fascinating books were selected and acquired by the same hand, assisted by the same eye.

In inspecting the large libraries I've mentioned (Alsop, Cairns, Sontag) one would guess within five minutes that these libraries had been *formed* by one intellect. The look of a reader's books on the shelf is a kind of signature, in my case suggesting that there's a certain style of bookmaking—or maybe several styles—and these somehow reinforce my desire to read a book.

I didn't form my library, though, for the look of the books on the shelf. I formed it to read and I've read it, though, in the cases of some literatures (German, for example) at a somewhat attenuated pace.

What about books that disappoint? Many do. These, in my life, fall into two classes: boring, turgid books that I'll never want to read; and interesting and worthy books whose hour has not yet come.

48

I SEE THAT once again I've strayed off from writing to reading and the seeking out of books to read. This might cause some readers to grow impatient: what, after all, does my attraction to certain binding styles have to do with writing—and writing, more or less, is what this book is supposed to be about. They have everything to do with my writing, but perhaps the seepage is aquifer-like: sponge-like the reading is slowly absorbed by the writing. Seeing my books reminds me that, in a modest way at least, I'm part of literature and the whole complicated cultural enterprise that is literature. I have tried to write books that belong with the books I have gathered and read. The process is far from simple. My thousands of books are mainly the work of minor writers such as myself. Minor writers provide the stitchery of literature. Besides, major writers often find themselves writing minor books. Major writers aren't major all the time, and minor writers occasionally write better than they normally do, sometimes producing a major book. The commonwealth of literature is complex, but a sense of belonging to it is an important feeling for a writer to have and to keep. Sitting with the immortals does not make one an immortal, but the knowledge that they're around you on their shelves does contribute something to one's sense of what one ought to try for. An attitude of respect for all the sheer work that's been done since scribes first began to scratch on clay tablets is a good thing to cultivate.

49

IN PRACTICAL TERMS it's rather rare that I lift something directly from a book in my library and use it as the basis for a book of money.

Rather rare, but not unique. I did just that when I wrote *Buffalo Girls*, the starting point of which was a book of letters from (maybe) Calamity Jane to her daughter, letters that were reprinted by a small feminist press in the 1970s.

They were very poignant letters from Calamity Jane to someone—perhaps the teenage girl she was sometimes seen with, in the gold fields and elsewhere. Calamity Jane herself was very likely either hermaphroditic or pseudo-hermaphroditic; in neither case would she have been able to conceive, an aspect that, to me, makes the whole sad story more poignant. (In *Buffalo Girls* the daughter is imaginary, though in the terrible film that was made from it the daughter is real and is raised by an English lord!)

It is rare for me to base a whole book on another book, as with *Buffalo Girls*. But it is quite common for me to lift a nugget from some book. I have read, for example, a good deal about Afghanistan in the time of the Great Game, which was largely a struggle between England and Russia over Central Asia and the land route to India.

Perhaps the most dramatic part of this story was the British army's terrible retreat from Kabul in 1842, during which they were virtually wiped out by the well-hidden marksmen of the hill tribes. There is a famous painting of the lone survivor, a Dr. Brydon, arriving at Jalalabad. The painting is called *The Last of Ten Thousand* and was much reprinted and circulated in the nineteenth century.

I use it in one scene in *Somebody's Darling* when my old screenwriter Joe Percy, author of many B and C movies, is attending an opening at Lincoln Center and imagines himself, amid the finery, the Dr. Brydon of B movie scribes. It takes a footnote now. The books of Peter Hopkirk and others have kept the Great Game alive, but some knowledge only trickles down so far—not too many would figure out or recognize where I got that scene.

50

ABOUT THREE YEARS ago I began to notice that the natural arc both of my reading and my writing was suffering what might be called an autumnal change. The change began to manifest itself as I was entering my seventies, an age that is not yet quite winter but is certainly no longer spring or summer.

Suddenly the tide seemed to be ebbing, although I continued to read and write at more or less my accustomed pace.

First, the balance of my writing seemed to have shifted from mostly fiction to mostly nonfiction. After *Duane's Depressed*—in my opinion my best novel—the one fictional effort that I really liked was *Loop Group*, my second Hollywood novel. By the time I wrote it I actually knew something about the place and gave a good accounting of it. (I also liked my final tetralogy, *The Berrybender Narratives*; but I seem to share these last enthusiasms with very few.)

Once the new century got underway I began mostly to occupy myself with nonfiction. This is in accordance with my long held belief that age doesn't favor the novelist. The poet Richard Howard and many others ridicule this point, but I remain wedded to it. There are, of course, exceptions—in the arts as in life there are exceptions. But, in the main, fiction's greatest achievements were made by the middle-aged.

Part of the problem, if there *is* a problem (rather than just a fixation of mine), is that the level of the writer's octane changes. It becomes harder and harder—or, at least, has with me—to produce the high burn that fiction needs.

I suppose this caveat needs to be taken with a grain of salt, since I keep saying I'm finishing up with fiction even as I allow myself another novel, and yet another. (The reason for this is not a desire to use up my last few drops of artistic testosterone; the reason for this is money—need of—which is seldom far from my mind; I suspect it's seldom far from most writers' minds. I said earlier that, thanks to the fortune-teller's conviction, the need of money seldom has determined my artistic decisions, which is to a point true. But the necessity of money nags. I like the feel of having a fresh book to sell, just in case.)

In the back of my mind it may be that I still keep General Custer handy, in a pinch. There's always room for another book on Custer, and someday, for some reason, I may end up writing one.

However solid and settled one's patterns and habits, when it comes to writing, the coming of age will generally force one to come up with variations: shortcuts, maybe, or long cuts: whatever seems likely to produce good writing.

Lately, spurred on by an excellent *New Yorker* piece by Louis Menand, I stood looking for a while at my shelves of fiction by American writers of the Sixties, Seventies, Eighties whom Mr. Menand calls, and who sometimes thought of themselves as, postmodernists. These would include William H. Gass, Robert Cover, John Barth, Donald Barthelme, Thomas Pynchon, Kurt Vonnegut, and a few others. Of these I think Pynchon produced the one true masterpiece—*V*—and there are quite a few short story masterpieces scattered among the lot, several of them by Donald

Barthelme, though, if I had to include only one story from these writers it would be William H. Gass's "The Pedersen Kid," which I included in my anthology *Still Wild*.

What I thought of Donald Barthelme, who produced about 150 short stories, is that his was a true artistic high-wire act. If his stories weren't perfect they were dead.

Perfection is not to be achieved every day; no one knew that better than Donald Barthelme. I suspect he got there maybe a dozen times in his short fiction, and wrote one novel, *The Dead Father*, that is still important. Like many writers of his time he tended toward Beckett as he got older—indeed, Beckett himself only became Beckett as he aged—his early fiction is quite florid, unlike the spare masterpieces of his great phase. Indeed the whole postmodernist school, if it *was* a school and if it *was* postmodern, had the problem of following Beckett, just as an earlier generation of prose writers had the problem of following Hemingway—and they knew it.

51

IN OLD AGE one writes, if at all, what one can. I don't know that I've changed my writing patterns or concerns so very much, but, once I found I was in my seventies, what I did change were my *reading* patterns.

For much of my life I have essentially read for adventure or intellectual need. I began knowing no history, literary or otherwise; now I know a fair amount. Surprises of a literary or intellectual nature have become less common. In fact, I slowly came to realize, I would now rather *reread* than read. In Tucson, where I mostly live and work, I have assembled a small library of books I reread—and keep rereading.

Prominent among them are the *Diaries* (in twelve volumes) of the minor English aesthete and man of letters James Lees-Milne, who died at the end of 1997 and had begun keeping his diary in 1942. When these books were suggested to me, by my friend John Saumarez Smith, then of Heywood Hill, James Lees-Milne was little read and little mentioned. I wrote a piece about him for *The New York Review of Books* which made him, in time, something of an industry. (That issue of the *NYRB* was shortly stolen from every men's club in London.) The *Diaries*, published over the decades by several publishers, are now in print in a classy paperback, and a biography is due this fall.

Meanwhile I have read the whole *Diary* at least eight times. Why is hard to say. I know few of the people Lees-Milne mentions and probably wouldn't like either his wife or much of his acquaintance, should I have made it.

And yet the *Diary* has for me immense charm. If I'm dining out I take a volume with me to dinner, and have been doing this for about a decade. I said in my piece that I thought they were as good as Pepys, which got me a slap on the wrist from John Gross.

My feeling is that Mr. Gross should take another look. Pepys, Kilvert, Virginia Woolf—Lees-Milne fits squarely in this company.

But my attachment to the *Diaries* signals a real shift in my needs as a reader: where once I read for adventure, now I read mainly for *security*.

When I sit down at dinner with a given book, I want to know what I'm going to find.

Do books occasionally fall off the list? Of course. I once enjoyed Harold Nicolson's *Journals*, but doubt I'll look at them again. But Janet Flanner's three volumes of reportage to *The New Yorker* from Paris remain fresh to me today—I find myself frequently dipping in.

Indeed, if I were to write a book or a long essay about various things I've read throughout my life, that would be the perfect title for it: *Dipping In.*

If reading patterns change in one's final decades, what about the changes in writing patterns?

In my case I feel that somehow I got away with three novels that I hadn't expected to write: *Loop Group, When the Light Goes,* and *Rhino Ranch*. Of these *Loop Group* is a book I had long wanted to write—a kind of love letter, really, to the working women of Hollywood, many of whom I've known and liked. The Hollywood of the guilds has been little noticed, and yet if it were not for the skilled guild workers even fewer good movies would ever get made.

My heroine, Maggie, lives on De Longpre Avenue in Hollywood—odd that I should make a second visit to De Longpre Avenue; in my first visit my gifted antique scout Cadillac Jack goes there to try and buy one of Rudolph Valentino's cobra hubcaps from an old woman who is so poor she uses piled-up telephone books as a table.

The two additions to the *Picture Show* books each came as a surprise. Despite the fact of *Horseman, Pass By* and *Leaving Cheyenne*, my first two novels, I somehow, internally, reckon the real beginning of my career as a fiction writer to be *The Last Picture Show* and, particularly, to the creation of Duane Moore, the small-town success who turns out to be the only character who appears in all five of these novels. His growing self-awareness sustains the last four of the five books.

Why so many tetralogies, followed now by a quintet? Perhaps it has something to do with Shakespeare's notion of the several ages of man. In Duane I've actually followed a character from late adolescence to final old age. Perhaps that's what I have always wanted to do, as a novelist. The urge to revisit characters at various stages of life is one I've always had, and Duane Moore, an uneducated working-class oilman, who nonetheless achieved involvements and attachments to several women who *were* educated and were not of the working class, seemed to be a character who could add scope ultimately to the ranch and small-town environment in which I was raised.

That said, I never thought of Duane as me. Except for a handful of passages—the chapters in *Duane's Depressed* that describe his depression—the books aren't autobiographical. He doesn't know what I know, despite having been forced by his analyst to read Proust.

But I know what he knows and tracing Duane's long evolution has been fascinating work.

*   *   *

When I finished *Rhino Ranch* I thought of it as a farewell to fiction. After all I have finally killed off the character who has occupied me the longest. Duane Moore was never as broadly popular as the two seemingly immortal Rangers of *Lonesome Dove*: Captains Woodrow Call and Augustus McCrae. But *Lonesome Dove* was at bottom a romance. The *Picture Show* quintet isn't. It's very old-fashioned solid realism, the very thing the postmodernists were determined to eliminate. (And yet they didn't.)

In most cases it's probably the Reaper, rather than the writer, who decides what the final book will be.

52

As energetic and committed a rereader as I am, the books that I find I have the most difficulty rereading—as I suggested earlier—are my own. Several times, while writing this commentary, I've felt that I ought to go down the whole long list of my books—about forty in number—and see what's what. And yet, when I pick up *Horseman, Pass By* or one of the other early books, I realize very soon that this is a book I just can't read. I have read most of them only in the specialized way in which you read something as you're writing it. No one, as far as I know, has gone very deeply into the question of how accurately a writer can read what he or she is writing as the writing is still in progress.

Henry James brushes up against this question—as he brushes up against practically everything having to do with fiction, but he doesn't worry about it much, mainly because he's too busy writing the next book or the next review. When Scribners offered him the New York Edition he got what few writers receive: a chance to revise, not his whole work but a very substantial part of it. And he changed much. But, by this time, he had his magisterial confidence and sailed right into a job that he could hardly have imagined he would ever get when he wrote the fiction in the first place.

I don't think, given the opportunity James had, that I could profitably revise my own work. I can adapt my work for the screen but I can't rework it on the page.

One of the reasons I'm the bane of copy editors is that I immediately lose interest in my work once it's finished. I give due diligence to the copyediting, but by the time the page proofs arrive my indifference has hardened and I can usually only focus long enough to catch the most egregious errors. (Other and better writers have had the same problem—Dickens and Balzac for two, but they were writing with the printer's boy waiting and lots of immediate bills to pay.)

I give more attention, usually, to my essays, but those I now do for *The New York Review of Books* come back with corrections or suggestions so minuscule that I can't read them, even with a magnifying glass. Since I can't see the queries I let that august paper clean up my submissions as best they can.

In certain famous cases—Proust and Joyce, for example—the additions and corrections scribbled in the margins are so profuse and confusing that I marvel that these masterpieces ever got printed in intelligible form at all. They did, but that's not the end of the textual disputes that have gathered around them, disputes that, like the editing of Shakespeare, may well continue for at least another century.

At the beginning of my career I was much concerned with prose style. I read Herbert Read's book on the subject and rummaged around a good bit in George Saintsbury's massive addresses to the subject. Though at first attracted to prose lyricists such as James Agee and William Styron (at least in *Lie Down in Darkness*), I soon realized I could not write lyrical prose in my fiction, and, after a bit, I ceased to want to. I developed a tiny theory, which is that a writer's prose should be be congruent with the landscape he is peopling. It made sense that Faulkner, from the deeply forested South, would write a dense and complex prose, whereas, say, Willa Cather, a plains state author, would write more sparely, as, in fact, I do myself. I'm frequently reminded that my way of looking at both life and art results from the fact that I grew up beneath the bounteous skies of the Great Plains. I write plainly and such few flourishes as I attempt are more apt to show up in my nonfiction, not my fiction.

One of the most famous critical comments of the twentieth century was made by the man of letters Cyril Connolly in his famous *Enemies of Promise*, where he divides prose writers into mandarins as opposed to those who work in the vernacular. Ronald Firbank is a perfect, if minor, mandarin, likewise Aldous Huxley, Virginia Woolf, and others.

Cyril Connolly, as a prose writer, mainly fell between the two camps. His aphoristic *The Unquiet Grave* is mandarin but his novel *The Rock Pool* and most of his reviewing, some of it very fine, is not. Connolly found and capitulated to not a few enemies of his own promise; he died largely unfulfilled and his lovely library is in Tulsa, beside Edmund Wilson's, which was not lovely. Edmund Wilson used his books and used them hard.

My prose models, aside from my attachment to *On the Road*, have never been American; after *On the Road* Kerouac himself simply opened the spigot and let his prose run and run, producing an ever higher percentage of sheer drivel.

I think the two prose models I would recommend to young writers are E. M. Forster and Evelyn Waugh, both of whom seldom published an unclear sentence. Waugh's *Sword of Honor* trilogy is a fine example of prose that gets the job done.

From the American tent I admire the workaday but forceful prose of Theodore Dreiser, and of course the brilliance and economy of Ernest Hemingway's *The Sun Also Rises* and the early stories. That book, as various writers have pointed out, is one of the most contagious of modern times. If you work in prose fiction and you read *The Sun Also Rises* it is very hard not to imitate it.

On the subject of prose, it was my hero James Lees-Milne who pointed out that there is something too clipped about the prose of Anthony Powell. Though grammatical to a fault, it is Powell's almost abbreviated sentences that cause the reader to read many sentences over, which perhaps Anthony Powell wants from us.

Lees-Milne published the remarks in a diary entry written (or, at least, published) after Powell was dead. And his complaints are nothing to the vinegar which Sir Vidia Naipaul poured on his old friend Anthony in a recent book, going so far as to suggest that if he had read the *Dance* a little sooner he and Powell might not have stayed friends at all. If one moves much in literary society it's dangerous to be picky about prose.

But, obviously, turning friends into enemies is sometimes part of the point.

53

WHAT SEEMS TO me true now is that Samuel Beckett was—from the Sixties on—as much imitated a master as Hemingway had been for the writers of the Twenties and Thirties. The plays of Beckett lie behind the plays of the late Harold Pinter; he lies behind most of the postmodernists I mentioned earlier, particularly the short fiction of Donald Barthelme.

In earlier times T. S. Eliot had this force of influence, but he mainly influenced poets and critics, not novelists or short story writers.

V. S. Naipaul is obviously a great writer, but his genius is mostly to manifest itself in his nonfiction, not his fiction. This is a touchy point with writers who consider themselves novelists first. Suggesting that their nonfiction is really better will usually be taken as a deadly insult. Yet I think it's true of James Baldwin, as well as Norman Mailer, none of whose novels equal the great "reportage" he did in the Sixties and Seventies. (The exception is his masterpiece, *The Executioner's Song*, which is so good that it doesn't matter which genre one puts it in.)

I like Cynthia Ozick's fiction but I like her brilliant essays even more.

And there are days when I think my own nonfiction will outlive my novels, mostly. *Walter Benjamin at the Dairy Queen* is as good as anything I've written, with the possible exception of *Duane's Depressed*.

*　　　*　　　*

One reason to stop writing fiction is to curb a writer's natural tendency to self-repetition. Long ago, in Jim Brown's writing class, I learned about something called incremental repetition: meaning, I guess, that every time you repeat something, be it only phrases, you should add a little something. Done right this increases the force of the scene you're trying to write. Incremental repetition? It sounds good and one would not have to look too far to find examples in prose fiction when it works.

Applied to sentences, repetitions are probably workable and effective; applied to scenes I'm not so sure. Norman Mailer once remarked somewhere that he had written about anal sex twice—and so what. The choice of what sort of thing to maybe repeat was to reinforce the so what? It's a little like repeating once too often the rumor that the Marquis de Sade may have expired while having sex with a goose. In our jaded day and time this might startle once or possibly even twice (to some innocents) but after twice you're diminishing, not incrementing, your anecdote.

Hemingway was a better repeater than his rival Gertrude Stein, but the masterwork of incremental repetition, if there is one, is Gertrude Stein's *The Making of Americans.* Janet Malcolm and John Ashbery are on record as having read it, plus a very small group of scholars. I once owned a copy that had belonged to a dentist in Baltimore. Whether he read it I don't know, and I sold it too quickly to read it myself.

What I have hoped to be, all my mature life, is a man of letters. Somerset Maugham, not much valued today, was a man of letters, and his valedictory statement is to be found in a lovely book called *The Summing Up,* which, in my youth, I read many times. Somerset Maugham was not the best writer of his age—neither was Arnold Bennett nor H. G. Wells, with which he is often classed—but he was a very competent, readable man of letters. He became rich and bought a fine villa in the South of France, where Winston Churchill and many other famous people came to dine. *The Summing Up* is an excellent, smart, seasoned description of how a man of letters lives and works.

These memoirs of my own, with a volume yet to come, are collectively *my* summing up. And what they sum up is how satisfying the work of a man of letters—I believe I now am one—can be.

Never discount luck, in the making of a literary career, or any other career, for that matter. I would probably have been a writer of some sort no matter what, but I would not so easily have been able to make a good life for myself and my son were it not for the lucky fact that my novels attracted, and still attract, good moviemakers, who caused them to yield good movies that were financially successful as well.

That's the sum of it, reader. Now it's on to the big adventure that is Hollywood.